# Contents

|  |  |
|---|---|
|  | 2 |
| Welcome | 3 |
| How to use this guide | 4 |
| Vouchers | 7 |
| Assessing the restaurants of Wales | 9 |
| Foods of Wales | 12 |
| Markets | 14 |
| Farm shops | 18 |
| Food festivals | 20 |
| True Taste Award winners | 24 |
| Entries | 30 |
| Index | 180 |
| Vote for your favourite restaurant | 184 |
| Report forms | 185 |
| Useful websites | 191 |
| Location map | 192 |

# Credits

Carlton House

Dining out in Wales 2005 is published by the
Welsh Development Agency
Plas Glyndŵr, Kingsway,
Cardiff CF10 3AH
Tel: 08457 775577
www.walesthetruetaste.com
© Copyright 2005
Welsh Development Agency
**Editor:** Simon Wright
**Inspections:** Simon Wright, Elizabeth Carter, David Hancock, Mark Manson, Sarah Peart, Jenny White
**Designed and produced by:** Peter Gill & Associates, Cardiff
**Photography by:** Huw Jones Advertising Photography, Newport
**Printed by:** MWL Print Group, Pontypool

Dining out in Wales accepts no payment for entries, advertising or free meals. The Welsh Development Agency (the 'WDA') reserves all rights it has in any intellectual property contained in this guide. No part of this guide may be reproduced, transmitted in any form or by any means or stored in any retrieval system of any nature without permission, except for permitted fair dealing under the Copyright, Designs and Patents Act 1988 or in accordance with the terms of an appropriate licence. Application for permission for other use of copyright material including permission to reproduce extracts in other published works shall be made to the publisher. Full acknowledgment of author, publisher and source must be given.

In all cases this guide is intended for guidance only and the WDA gives no warranty, either expressed or implied, as to the accuracy of any data used by the WDA in preparing this guide or as to any other data set out or opinions expressed in this guide.

Except for any misrepresentation made fraudulently, the WDA does not accept any liability (whether in contract, tort (including negligence), breach of statutory duty, restitution or otherwise) for any loss or damage (including, without limitation, consequential loss, loss of business or profits, depletion of goodwill and like loss) arising in any way whether directly or indirectly out of or in connection with the use of or reliance on this guide or for any defect or error in this guide.

# Welcome

## Editor Simon Wright

When I first became aware of the possibility of an independent guide to eating out in Wales I greeted the prospect with genuine excitement. At the time I had just finished a stint as editor of a UK wide guide to dining out and, whilst I had always been an enthusiastic advocate of restaurants in my home country, I was also aware that as a matter of simple geography, guides based in the South East of England struggle to do justice to eating out in Wales. An independently inspected guide dedicated solely to Welsh restaurants was long overdue.

The principal purpose of a guide book should simply be to help the reader eat well. Whether it's Milan, Madrid, New York, Paris or Sydney, you can eat badly anywhere in the world if you don't know where to go. It follows then that if we want to give the best impression of eating out in Wales then we need to do all we can to identify the finest places to eat and draw them to the attention of the public.

This book was the result of around 200 unannounced and independent inspections that took place in a three month period across the length and breadth of Wales by a team of experienced reviewers. There is no payment taken for entry in this guide and all meals are paid for at the time of the visit. Any honest food critic will tell you that this is not a wholly scientific process and whilst those carrying out the visits are trained to look for the same qualities in every meal (and you can find out just what they were looking for in Assessing the Restaurants of Wales, see page 9) their experience is inevitably a snapshot. You may agree or disagree with our findings but in many ways that is part of the point – if your experience doesn't reflect what's in the guide or you think we've overlooked some culinary gem then we want to hear from you (see Vote For Your Favourite Restaurant on page 184). If this book gets people talking about eating out, inspires them in their search for new restaurants and encourages them to support the many excellent places to eat in Wales, then it will have done its job.

# How to use this guide

**Contact details** — Nefyn Road, Pwllheli, Gwynedd LL53 5TH
Tel: 01758 612363
Email: gunna@bodegroes.co.uk
www.bodegroes.co.uk
On Nefyn Road (A497), one mile west of Pwllheli

**Name** — Plas Bodegroes
**Location** — Pwllheli
**Award level**

**Description** — Whichever way you look at it, this fine Georgian country house impresses both for its décor and for its professional service. The look is cool, minimal, tasteful, especially so in the dining room where modern lighting and wall-to-wall contemporary art are deployed with panache. Chris Chown's food moves with the times and seasons, uses local produce to good effect and offers a few luxuries that the surroundings demand, such as briefly seared foie gras and pigeon breast with an outstanding pigeon pastilla. A high degree of workmanship characterises much of the cooking, seen in a delicate mousseline of scallop, crab and laverbread with a well-judged crab sauce, and a stand-out rosemary kebab of mountain lamb with accompaniments of courgette provençale and garlic potatoes throwing the whole dish into sharp relief. Impressive desserts may include rich cardamom crème brûlée teamed with poached pears, while rhubarb and apple are sandwiched between cinnamon biscuits and served with elderflower custard. The wine list roams far and wide, taking in many fine producers, yet prices are remarkably restrained.

**True Taste award** — True Taste hospitality Gold 2002-3

**Details text & symbols** — Owners: Chris & Gunna Chown Chef: Chris Chown Open: L Sun 12.00 – 2.30 D Tues – Sat 7.00 – 9.30 Closed: Mid-Dec-Jan Seats: 40
L £17.50 D £38
16 11 P
Visa/MastercardSwitch/Delta Map reference **122**

**Map reference**

151

**Sample entry**

## Finding a restaurant

### By name
If you're looking for a particular restaurant then refer to the index on page 180 where you'll find all the establishments included in the guide listed alphabetically.

### By location
Consult the map at the back of the guide. All the restaurants included in the guide are featured on the map with a number in a red circle. This corresponds to a number (also in a red circle) to be found at the bottom of each entry.

## Reading an entry

### The award level
The box of colour at the top of each page indicates the level of award achieved by the restaurant featured on that page. The awards are Bronze, Silver, Gold and Gold Star (indicated by the presence of a star symbol situated within the gold box). An explanation of what each level means can be found on page 9.

### Location and contact details
At the top of the entry you will find the address of the establishment and a telephone number together with email and web details where available. Below these you will generally find a brief line of simple directions.

### The description
The middle section of the entry describes the restaurant and gives an impression of what you might expect should you decide to dine there. Depending on the character of the venue, you will find comments on the surroundings, the food, the service and the wine list.

### The details
At the bottom of the page you will find a wealth of information about the restaurant contained in a combination of text and symbols.

### Head chef/owners
The first few lines give the name of the head chef or chefs) and the owners at the time of going to press.

### Open
This is followed by the opening hours as supplied to us by the establishment. L indicates lunch and D indicates dinner. Opening times are always liable to be changed and it is always wise to phone and check before making a special journey.

### Closed
This indicates any period of annual closing as indicated to us by the establishment.

### Prices 🍴
The prices indicate the average cost of a three-course meal at lunch and dinner.
These figures are supplied by the establishment and may sometimes relate to the price of a set-price menu rather than the à la carte.

*How to use this guide*

# How to use this guide

2

The establishment has accommodation (number of rooms indicated).

There is free parking onsite or within easy reach of the restaurant.

There is independent wheelchair access to both the main restaurant and the toilets.

There is wheelchair access to both the main restaurant and the toilets with assistance.

Vegetarians are catered for.

Children are welcome (an r after this symbol indicates that there are some restrictions and you should check with the restaurant).

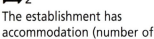

The establishment uses some organic produce.

Special diets are catered for (usually by prior arrangement).

Smoking is not allowed anywhere inside the establishment.

Smoking is only allowed in designated areas.

Smoking allowed in all areas.

Outside dining available in fine weather.

40

Private parties. Maximum number indicated.

These credit cards accepted.

Dining out in Wales vouchers can be used at this establishment (see page 7 for details).

# Vouchers

## Dining out in Wales 2005
## £5 voucher

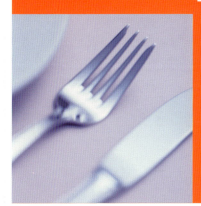

Valid at participating establishments as indicated in Dining out in Wales 2005.

For Terms and Conditions of offer please see overleaf.

**Offer valid until 1 November 2005**

## Dining out in Wales 2005
## £5 voucher

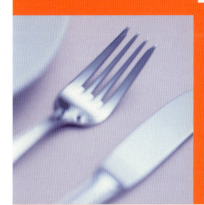

Valid at participating establishments as indicated in Dining out in Wales 2005.

For Terms and Conditions of offer please see overleaf.

**Offer valid until 1 November 2005**

# Vouchers

**Terms and Conditions**

- This voucher may be used at participating establishments denoted by 🏠 on some entries in Dining out in Wales 2005.
- Only original vouchers issued with this guide are valid. Photocopies or other reproductions will not be accepted.
- This voucher may not be used in conjunction with any other promotion.
- Only one voucher may be used per table booked.
- This voucher may be redeemed against the cost of a meal for two or more people subject to a minimum spend of £20 per person (inclusive of drinks, VAT and service).
- This voucher cannot be exchanged for cash and has no monetary value.
- Use of this voucher is subject to participating establishments terms and conditions.
- Please ask for details in advance of dining.

---

**Terms and Conditions**

- This voucher may be used at participating establishments denoted by 🏠 on some entries in Dining out in Wales 2005.
- Only original vouchers issued with this guide are valid. Photocopies or other reproductions will not be accepted.
- This voucher may not be used in conjunction with any other promotion.
- Only one voucher may be used per table booked.
- This voucher may be redeemed against the cost of a meal for two or more people subject to a minimum spend of £20 per person (inclusive of drinks, VAT and service).
- This voucher cannot be exchanged for cash and has no monetary value.
- Use of this voucher is subject to participating establishments terms and conditions.
- Please ask for details in advance of dining.

# Assessing the restaurants of Wales

Everyone who eats out is a food critic. We all have our own views on the restaurants we visit and the food we eat there. People's views differ of course, partly because of personal taste and partly because it's possible to have a quite different experience in the same restaurant. So how is it possible to make a guide of this type meaningful in terms of the awards that it bestows upon the places included?

The only answer to that question lies in ensuring that the team of inspectors are working to a set of clear criteria by which they assess the places that they visit.

This doesn't mean that they are looking for a particular style of cooking or expecting to find specific dishes on the menu at any one restaurant. Those are decisions for chefs and owners and it is obvious that their aim must be to satisfy their customers before anybody else.

It is though possible to identify the key factors that are widely accepted to contribute to good cooking (whatever the style of restaurant) and it is these that form the backbone of the criteria for the awards in Dining out in Wales.

## The Criteria

**The True Taste brand celebrates Wales as the home of a modern food culture. It is built on authenticity, purity and quality and its brand values are integrity, expertise, naturalness and pleasure. Overall, Dining out in Wales restaurants should reinforce the True Taste message and offer a pleasurable experience for consumers.**

**Bronze**
Ingredients will be carefully selected for quality with an emphasis on using fresh local produce. With minor exceptions most elements of the meal will be produced in the establishments own kitchen. Technical skills, timing, seasoning and the balancing of flavours will be competently handled. Dishes will be presented with care. Service will be prompt and enthusiastic.

# Assessing the restaurants of Wales

### Silver
The kitchen will display a clear commitment to obtaining and employing the very best of fresh ingredients with an emphasis on local, seasonal produce. With few exceptions, all elements of the meal will be produced in the establishment's own kitchen. Technical skills, timing, seasoning and the balancing of flavours will be generally accurate. There will be an obvious understanding of classic techniques. Dishes will be presented with care and skill. Service will be attentive, well informed and enthusiastic.

### Gold
Establishments will demonstrate a dedication to sourcing the best ingredients available with obvious attention having been paid to seasonality and the seeking out of top local produce. It is likely that all elements of the meal will be produced in the establishment's own kitchen including stocks and patisserie. Technical skills, timing, seasoning and the balancing of flavours will be precise. There will be an element of innovation and a distinctive cooking style. Service will be professional, knowledgeable and enthusiastic.

### Gold Star
The cooking will be of the very highest standard available in Wales and will compare favourably with the standards achieved in the best-rated establishments in Britain as a whole and more widely in Europe. Chefs will be committed to sourcing the highest quality ingredients available in the marketplace and are likely to highlight the use of local ingredients of the very finest international standards. It is unlikely that these kitchens will buy in any pre-prepared produce whatsoever. Technical skills, timing, seasoning and the balancing of flavours will be flawless. The cooking will be informed, innovative and highly evolved in style. Service standards will equate with that offered in Britain's most highly regarded establishments.

## What the inspectors look for

### 1. Quality of ingredients
Good cooking begins with good shopping. Whatever the skills of the kitchen, few will have the capacity to turn lead

Owens

into gold and it is therefore the quality of the ingredients, more than any other factor, that will dictate the success of a finished dish.

## 2. Accuracy and timing

Once good produce has been sourced, the next task is to cook it with care. Respect and sympathy for the basic raw materials are at the root of all good cooking and this demands an understanding of which techniques are suited to bringing out the best in a particular item of produce.

## 3. Balance of flavours

Combining ingredients and flavours on a plate to create a harmonious whole is one of the biggest challenges for any kitchen. Too often chefs fall prey to the lure of over complication when the truth is that in cooking (as in many other things) less often means more.

## 4. Presentation

Good presentation does not necessarily mean food being heavily worked by many pairs of hands. It's important to keep in mind that dishes that comprise good fresh ingredients in intelligent combinations, accurately cooked, will by their very nature tend to look good. Putting things on a plate simply for presentational reasons is unlikely to result in a more successful dish.

## 5. Innovation

Novelty, as far as cooking goes, is not an end in itself and simply trying something new will not in itself make for a successful dish – it has to work.

## 6. Service

Surveys indicate that the quality of service at a restaurant is at least important to the customer as the quality of the food. However, the same studies show that it is not fussy service that customers seek, but competent, friendly service.

## 7. Other factors

There are of course other elements, most notably ambience, that will also influence the customer's enjoyment of a meal. In Dining out in Wales these matters are dealt with in the description that an establishment receives, so that the reader can get a sense of the style and atmosphere of a particular restaurant.

# Foods of Wales

## Home cooking

**In Wales the phrase 'locally produced' is so synonymous with quality that chefs rarely need to look far for great ingredients.** *Jenny White* **takes us on a whistle stop tour of their local larder.**

Welsh produce is as rich and varied as the landscape – the yield of a land of lazy rolling countryside, dark commanding hills, gentle rivers and dramatic coastlines. The latter provides a daily bounty of peerless seafood – fish and crustaceans at ports as bustling as Milford Haven or as timeless as Solva; oysters, mussels and clams from the Menai Straits and shellfish from Cardigan Bay or the Gower Peninsula, whose famous cockles are traditionally eaten with the inky seaweed delicacy of laverbread.

Move inland and you'll find the fields are grass green rather than corn gold. A broad swathe of pasture runs from South to West Wales, nourishing one of the densest dairy areas in Europe. 70% of the milk produced in West Wales stays there and most of it goes into cheese making. Cheese making in Wales has become a real passion amongst small producers and it is home to some of the finest cheeses currently being made in Britain with a wonderful range on offer.

Way out west in Pembrokeshire, where low roofed cottages are lashed by sea winds, the fertile ground yields potatoes from May to August and a variety of fruit and vegetables are grown with success and it's a similar story in South Wales, thanks to a mild climate and high rainfall. The area also supports a number of wine growers – a tradition that dates back to Roman times and was resurrected in the 1970s. In the extreme north, on Anglesey everything from fruit to grain is farmed and the yields are so high that the island is affectionately dubbed Mon Mam Cymru, the Mother of Wales.

Beef farming has been well documented in Wales since the time of the Celts. Excellent grazing pastures and a high proportion of traditional breeds ensure a quality product. Where the land becomes steeper, hardy Welsh Black cattle thrive. The oldest breed in the UK, they are

renowned for their flavour-packed, marbled meat. Move higher still, and the hills are dotted with sheep. Welsh Lamb is in plentiful supply throughout the year. Even in the shadowy heart of North Wales, where the mountains seem to sprout only shards of slate, sheep eke out a living on wild herbs and grasses, the diet lending their meat a distinctive sweetness. On the soft coastal marches, from the Llŷn Peninsula to the Severn Estuary, the saline tides lend salt marsh lamb its fine, delicate flavour.

Water flows freely in Wales, tumbling in silver ribbons across the land. There are countless suppliers of spring water and the farming of fish – trout in particular – is flourishing. Rare Arctic char are caught in the deep, dark lakes of Snowdonia, salmon thrive in the river Dovey and the Wye provides both salmon and elvers. In West Wales the Towy, Teifi and Cleddau are famous for the princely sewin (sea trout). The coracle – a keel-less, bowl shaped fishing boat – has been used in Wales for centuries. Once seen as the poachers' vehicle of choice, their owners were described in an 1863 report of Her Majesty's Inspector of Salmon Fisheries as 'often lawless and always aggressive...difficult to detect and almost impossible to capture'. Coracles are still used on the Teifi and the river Towy, which winds through a land of broken castles past the county town of Carmarthen, where the beautifully dense and salty dry-cured ham is made.

All this just scratches the surface of the countless unique treasures produced in Wales. We haven't even touched upon smoked meats and fish, chocolates, preserves, waffles, a single malt whisky, a healthy number of independently brewed beers and of course some decadent ice creams, including those made by the descendants of the Italians who emigrated to the Welsh Valleys in the 1930s.

The best cooking is often that which bears the imprint of its location and of the seasons. As you browse through the pages of this book and visit the restaurants contained within it, you'll find that increasingly Welsh cooking is finding its own distinctive voice by doing just that.

# Markets

## Farmer's Markets of Wales

Local produce for local people underpins the ethos of Farmer's Markets. Regular markets take place throughout Wales. There are weekly fortnightly and monthly markets with their own particular characteristics and local flavours.

Seasonal vegetables, often harvested on that morning, are a regular feature as is the best of Welsh cheese, poultry, fresh meat and meat products. Loyal customers regularly buy from their favourite producers because they have every confidence that they get a fresher and better tasting product.

You can get information about the nearest Farmer's Market by logging on to the web site www.farmersmarketsinwales.co.uk. This site is hosted by the organisation responsible for co-ordinating support, marketing, providing training and regulating markets in Wales.

## South East Wales

**Abergavenny**
**Date** 4th Saturday each month
**Venue** Market Hall
**Contact** Margaret Wilding
**Tel** 01873 860271

**Caerphilly**
**Date** 2nd Saturday each month
**Venue** Twyn Community Centre
**Contact** Stacy Hardwick
**Tel** 01443 864314

**Cardiff**
**Date** Every Sunday
**Venue** Fitzhammon Embankment
**Contact** Ken Moon
**Tel** 029 2019 0036

**Chepstow**
**Date** 2nd & 4th Saturday each month
**Venue** Senior Citizens Centre
**Contact** Sarah Smith
**Tel** 01291 650672

**Cowbridge**
**Date** 1st Saturday each month
**Venue** A John's Car Park
**Contact** Norman Jenkins
**Tel** 01446 774036

**Penarth**
**Date** 3rd Saturday each month
**Venue** Conservative Club
**Contact** Norman Jenkins
**Tel** 01446 774036

**Porthcawl**
**Date** 4th Saturday each month
**Venue** Arwel y Mor
**Contact** Robert Lee
**Tel** 07793 393706

**Usk**
**Date** 1st & 3rd Saturday each month
**Venue** Memorial Hall
**Contact** Stephen Sherman
**Tel** 01600 869037

## West Wales

**Carmarthen**
**Date** 1st Friday each month
**Venue** Town Centre
**Contact** Nick Thomas
**Tel** 01269 590218

**Fishguard**
**Date** Saturday each fortnight
**Venue** Town Hall
**Contact** Andy Crook
**Tel** 01239 841827

**Haverfordwest**
**Date** Friday each fortnight
**Venue** Riverside Quay
**Contact** Kate Morgan
**Tel** 01437 776168

**Llandovery**
**Date** 4th Saturday each month
**Venue** Castle Hotel
**Contact** Dawn Hoare-Ward
**Tel** 01550 720369

**Mumbles**
**Date** 2nd Saturday each month
**Venue** British Legion Car Park
**Contact** Robin Bonham
**Tel** 01792 405169

## Mid Wales

**Aberystwyth**
**Date** 1st & 3rd Saturday each month
**Venue** North Parade
**Contact** Jan Fenner
**Tel** 01970 633066

**Brecon**
**Date** 2nd Saturday each month
**Venue** Market Hall
**Contact** Fiona Jones
**Tel** 01874 610008

**Cardigan**
**Date** 2nd & 4th Thursday each month
**Venue** Market Guidhall
**Contact** Jan Fenner
**Tel** 01970 633066

**Knighton**
**Date** 4th Saturday each month
**Venue** Community Centre
**Contact** Kevin Kell
**Tel** 01547 528011

**Lampeter**
**Date** 2nd & 4th Friday each month
**Venue** Market Street
**Contact** Jan Fenner
**Tel** 01970 633066

**Llandrindod Wells**
**Date** Last Thursday each month
**Venue** Middleton Street
**Contact** Michael Bleese
**Tel** 01597 824102

# Markets

*Farmer's Markets of Wales*

**Rhayder**
**Date** 2nd Thursday each month
**Venue** Market
**Contact** Wendy Abel
**Tel** 01597 810081

**Welshpool**
**Date** 1st Friday each month
**Venue** Town Hall
**Contact** Mark Jarvis
**Tel** 01686 670722

## North Wales

**Bangor**
**Date** Sunday each fornight
**Venue** Safeway Car Park
**Contact** Joanna Robertson
**Tel** 01248 421661

**Celyn**
**Date** 3rd Sunday each month
**Venue** North Wales College of Horticulture
**Contact** Ericka Mackie
**Tel** 01352 703217

**Colwyn Bay**
**Date** Each Thursday
**Venue** Bay View Shopping Centre
**Contact** Tudor Jones
**Tel** 01492 680209

**Wrexham**
**Date** 3rd Friday each month
**Venue** Queen Square
**Contact** Kenneth Barney
**Tel** 01978 292448

## Great indoor markets in Wales

Indoor markets are a feature at the heart of many of the towns and cities of Wales. Historically royal charters to trade exclusively were granted, some dating back to the twelfth century. The markets offer a vibrant mix of fresh food and general products and feature independent traders who pride themselves on delivering quality produce at a reasonable price.

The famous Swansea Market with its cockles, laver bread and fresh fish landed daily also has locally produced bread, such as the Swansea batch, as well as numerous butchers selling Welsh Lamb and beef. Local growers bring their vegetables in season from the Gower Peninsula to complete the colourful picture. Abergavenny is regarded as a market town with traders spilling out from the Market Hall into two of the town's main car parks and a range of non-food markets taking place throughout the week.

Newport Market has recently been revitalised through a major refurbishment and

# Indoor Markets of Wales

Cardiff market features a wide selection of fish and shellfish with numerous butchers selling game, salt marsh lamb and Welsh Black beef. Carmarthen market has many unique products ranging from farmhouse cheese, such as Teifi, to locally caught salmon, Carmarthen ham and Welsh salt bacon. Wrexham has three markets throughout the town including a Butcher's and People's Market and the biggest market in Wales is held in Neath, and has become famous for its faggots and peas! Smaller markets, such as Brecon, Pontypridd and Aberdare also provide a valuable service to their local communities.

**Aberdare**
Market Hall, Market Street
**Days** Monday – Saturday

**Abergavenny**
Town Hall, Cross Street
**Days** Tuesday, Friday and Saturday

**Brecon**
Market Hall, Market Street
**Days** Monday – Saturday

**Bridgend**
Rhiw Shopping Centre
**Days** Monday – Saturday

**Cardiff**
Central Market, St Mary Street
**Days** Monday – Saturday

**Carmarthen**
St Catherine Street
**Days** Monday – Saturday

**Llanelli**
Llanelli Market Hall
**Days** Monday – Saturday

**Neath**
Green Street
**Days** Monday – Saturday

**Newport**
High Street
**Days** Monday – Saturday

**Pontypool**
Market Street
**Days** Monday – Saturday

**Pontypridd**
Market Street
**Days** Wednesday, Friday and Saturday

**Swansea**
Oxford Street
**Days** Monday – Saturday

**Welshpool**
Town Hall, Broad Street
**Days** Monday and Saturday

**Wrexham**
Chester Street
**Days** Monday – Saturday

# Farm shops

Many small to medium sized farms now sell direct to the public. Where better to buy fresh, local, seasonal and traceable food than at the farm gate? Farm shops will generally sell produce reared and prepared on the farm as well as a range of local specialities.

## South and Mid Wales

**Brooks Farm**
Farm Shop in Raglan Village
High Street, Raglan,
Monmouthshire NP15 2DY
Tel: 01291 690319
Own beef, lamb and turkeys, free-range eggs. Local speciality foods and vegetables.

**Caws Cenarth**
Glyneithinog, Pontseli, Boncath
Carmarthenshire SA37 0LH
Award winning Welsh cheese.
Tel: 01239 710432

**Dyffryn Smoked Produce**
Beili-Mawr Home Farm
Dyffryn, Cardiff
Tel: 029 2059 9488
Smokers of bacon and fish.

**Glan Usk Farm**
Llanfair Kilgeddin Abergavenny,
Monmouthshire NP7 9YE
Tel: 07974 764919 (M)
Tel: 01873 880599
In season vegetables and fruit, lamb, local honey and apple juice.

**Tredilion Fruit Farm**
Llantilio Pertholey,
Abergavenny, Monmouthshire
NP7 8BG
Tel: 01873 854355
In season fruit and vegetables.

**Graig Farm Organics**
Dolau, Llandrindod Wells, Powys
Tel: 01597 851655
Wide range of meats, fish, home cured bacon, hams, ready meals and bread.

**Llangloffan Farmhouse Cheese Centre**
Castle Morris, Fishguard,
Pembrokeshire SA62 5ET
Tel: 01348 891241
Award winning cheeses.

**Llwynhelyg Farm Shop**
Sarnau, Llandysul, Ceredigion
Tel: 01239 811079
Wide range of home-grown vegetables, herbs and salad.

**M & D Embury**
Cadfor Farm, Govilon,
Abergavenny,
Monmouthshire NP7 9NU
Tel: 01743 853019
Beef and lamb, home cured bacon, pies and pasties, sponges and cakes.

**Medhope Organic Growers**
Tintern, Chepstow,
Monmouthshire NP16 7NX
Tel: 01291 680101
Fruit and vegetables.

Drovers Rest

**Pencrugiau Organic Farm Shop**
Pencrugiau, Velindre Farchog,
Crymych, Pembrokeshire
SA41 3XH
Tel: 01239 881265
A wide range of organic vegetables, salads and fruit.

**Penllyn Estate Farm**
Llwynhelig, Cowbridge,
Vale of Glamorgan
Tel: 01446 772600
Aberdeen Angus beef.

**Priory Farm Shop**
Priory Farm, New Hedges,
Tenby, Pembrokeshire SA70 8TN
Tel: 01834 844662
Fruit and home grown vegetables, baked goods, eggs, preserves.

**The Fruit Garden**
Groesfaen Road,
Peterson-Super-Ely, Cardiff
Tel: 01446 760358
Soft fruits, honey, free-range eggs and ice cream.

**Welsh Haven Products**
Whitegates Farm,
Little Haven, Haverfordwest,
Pembrokeshire
Tel: 01437 781552
Organic Farm Shop, chicken, poultry and geese.

**Wendy Brandon Preserves**
Felin Wen, Boncath,
Pembrokeshire SA37 0JR
Tel: 01239 841568
150 different varieties of preserves.

## North Wales

**Bellis Country Market**
Wrexham Road Farm,
Holt, Near Wrexham
Tel: 01829 270304
Fruit and vegetables, cheese and dairy products.

**Glasfryn Activity Park**
Glasfryn Fawr Farm,
Pencaenewydd, Pwllheli,
Gwynedd
Tel: 01766 810204
A wide range of farm goods.

**Gwydryn Hir**
Brynsiencyn, Anglesey
Tel: 01248 430344
Beef, lamb, pork, bacon, sausages, free-range eggs, soft fruit and vegetables, preserves.

**Yew Tree Farm**
Wrexham Road, Hope,
Wrexham
Tel: 01978 762151
Vegetables and autumn bedding plants.

**Rhug Organic Farm**
Corwen, Denbighshire
Tel: 01490 413000
Organic beef and lamb, pies, pasties and bread.

# Food Festivals
## 26 March – 17 December 2005

**Wales today has a vibrant food culture which is reflected in the many food festivals which take place across the country throughout the year. Festivals are a great opportunity to taste, talk about and buy the best local produce available directly from the farmer or food producer.**

26 March 2005
**St Clear's Festival of Food and Culture**
Venue/Location: St Clears Town Centre and West Wales Centre for the Crafts
Contact: Glyn Evans on 01994 230003

2 & 3 April 2005
**Llanwrtyd Wells Gourmet Festival of Fine Food and Drink**
Venue/Location: Bromsgrove Hall & Fields, Llanwrtyd Wells
Contact: Peter James on 01591 610264

28 May 2005
**Llanidloes Celtic Food Festival**
Venue/Location: Minerva Arts Centre, High Street, Llanidloes
Contact: Nick Davies on 01938 555893

28 – 30 May 2005
**Welsh Cider Festival**
Venue/Location: Clytha Arms, Near Abergavenny, Monmouthshire
Contact: Alan Golding on 029 2019 8206

10 – 12 June 2005
**Merlin, Magic and Mystery**
Venue/Location: Carmarthen Town Centre
Contact: Huw Parsons on 01554 747500

18 & 19 June 2005
**The Welsh Game Fair**
Venue/Location: Gelli Aur, Llandeilo, Carmarthenshire
Contact: Elvin Thomas on 01267 290519

25 June 2005
**Gwyl Fwyd Llandysul Food Festival**
Venue/Location: Llandysul Park
Contact: Ann Jones on 01559 362403

25 June 2005
**Hay-on-Wye Food Festival**
Venue/Location: Hay-on-Wye Primary School
Contact: Andrew Powell on 01874 624979

25 June – 3 July 2005
**Pembrokeshire Fish Week**
Venue/Location: Various throughout Pembrokeshire
Contact: Kate Morgan on 01437 776168

2 & 3 June 2005
**Newtown Multicultural Food Festival**
Venue/Location: The Park, Newtown
Contact: Shirley Owen on 01686 623538

1 & 2 July 2005
**Gwyl Fwyd Môr Llyn Seafood Festival**
Venue/Location: Nanhoron Hotel, Nefyn, Gwynedd
Contact: Owi Roberts on 07768 647670

8 – 10 July 2005
**Cardiff International Food and Drink Festival**
Venue/Location: Roald Dahl Plas (formerly the Oval Basin), Cardiff Bay
Contact: Connect to Cardiff on 029 2087 2987

18 – 21 July 2005
**The Royal Welsh Show**
Venue/Location: Royal Welsh Showground, Llanelwedd
Contact: Sarah Galloway on 029 2082 8945

23 July 2005
**The Lampeter Food Festival**
Venue/Location: University of Wales, Lampeter Campus
Contact: Hazel Thomas on 01570 423981

30 – 31 July 2005
**The Big Cheese**
Venue/Location: Caerphilly
Contact: Stacy Hardwick on 01443 864314

6 August 2005
**Celtica Food Festival**
Venue/Location: Celtica, Machynlleth
Contact: Nick Davies on 01938 555893

7 August 2005
**Aberaeron Food and Craft Fair at the Festival of Welsh Ponies and Cobs**
Contact: Jan Fenner on 01970 633066

10 & 11 August 2005
**United Counties Food Extravaganza**
Venue/Location: United Counties Showground, Carmarthen
Contact: Jackie Keen on 01267 232141

16 – 18 August 2005
**Pembrokeshire Agricultural Show**
Venue/Location: Withybush Showground, Haverfordwest, Pembrokeshire
Contact: Kate Morgan on 01437 776168

Food Festivals

# Food Festivals
## 26 March – 17 December 2005

18 August 2005
**Denbigh and Flint Agricultural Show**
Venue/Location: Showground, Denbigh Green
Contact: Catrin Jones on 01824 705802

27 & 28 August 2005
**Talgarth Festival of the Black Mountains**
Venue/Location: Based in The Square and throughout the town of Talgarth.
Contact: Barbara Christopher on 01874 712081

27 – 29 August 2005
**Brecon Beacons Summer Fayre**
Venue/Location: National Park Visitor Centre, Libanus, Brecon
Contact: Andrew Powell on 01874 624979

30 August 2005
**Frenni Food and Craft Fair**
Venue/Location: Crymych
Contact: Kevin Davies on 01239 831455

9 September 2005
**Harvest Fayre, Haverfordwest Farmers' Market**
Venue/Location: Riverside Quay Shopping Centre, Haverfordwest
Contact: Kate Morgan on 01437 776168

24 September 2005
**Rhayader Food Festival**
Venue/Location: Rhayader Leisure Centre
Contact: Nick Davies on 01938 555893

17 September 2005
**Aberystwyth Food and Craft Fayre 2004**
Venue/Location: Baker Street, Aberystwyth
Contact: Jan Fenner on 01970 633066

17 & 18 September 2005
**Abergavenny Food Festival**
Venue/Location: Abergavenny town centre, Monmouthshire
Contact: Julia French on 01873 851643

23 – 25 September 2005
**Narberth Food Festival**
Venue/Location: Queens Hall, Narberth
Contact: Mrs J Parfitt on 01834 860268 or Peter Preece on 01834 869364

1 October 2005
**Brecon Beacons Food Festival**
Venue/Location: Market Hall, Brecon, Powys
Contact: Andrew Powell on 01874 624979

## Food Festivals

**15 & 16 October 2005**
**Llangollen Food Festival**
Venue/Location: International Pavilion, Llangollen
Contact: Catrin Jones on 01824 705802

**22 & 23 October 2005**
**Gwyl Fwyd Conwy Food Festival**
Venue/Location: Various venues in Conwy
Contact: Jane Hughes on 01492 581600/ 0771 888 7478

**12 & 13 November 2005**
**Wrexham Food Festival**
Venue/Location: NEWI Sports Centre, Wrexham
Contact: Niall Waller on 01978 298381

**19 November 2005**
**Welshpool Winter Food Festival**
Venue/Location: Powys Suite at the Royal Oak Hotel, Welshpool
Contact: Nick Davies on 01938 555893

**26 November 2005**
**Brecon Beacons Christmas Fayre**
Venue/Location: Hay-on-Wye Memorial Car Park
Contact: Andrew Powell on 01874 624979

**26 November 2005**
**Wales Food Fair**
Venue/Location: Aberystwyth Arts Centre
Contact: Tamsin Wright on 01970 622889

**28 & 29 November 2005**
**The Royal Welsh Winter Fair**
Venue/Location: Royal Welsh Showground, Llanelwedd
Contact: Bob Morgan on 029 2082 8989

**2 – 4 December 2005**
**Saundersfoot St. Nicholas Fair**
Venue/Location: Saundersfoot Harbour, Saundersfoot
Contact: Andrew Evans on 01834 812304

**17 December 2005**
**Aberystwyth Christmas Food and Craft Fayre**
Venue/Location: Baker Street, Aberystwyth
Contact: Jan Fenner on 01970 633066

# True Taste/Gwir Flas
## Wales Food and Drink Awards 2004 – 5

**The True Taste/Gwir Flas Wales Food and Drink Awards celebrate and reward the food industry's most inspiring techniques and tastes.**

Now in their third year the awards are regarded as the 'gold standard' among food and drink producers in Wales. A UK renowned panel of judges from food writers to chefs, food inspectors and mystery shoppers, tasted and sampled the entries to sign post you to the very best.

We would like to thank our sponsors:
ASDA
ITV Wales
Hybu Cig Cymru/Meat Promotion Wales
The Grocer
and supporters:
Capper & Co Ltd/Spar, National Farmers' Union Cymru and the Farmers' Union of Wales.

### Ambassador of the Year
Rufus Carter
The Patchwork Traditional Food Company, Llys Parcwr, Ruthin, Denbighshire LL15 1NJ
Tel: 01824 705832
Rufus joined Patchwork – which was founded by his mother Margaret – 15 years ago and is now the company's managing director.

## True Taste Producer
For added value farm products produced by farmers and growers.

### Gold
Trethowan's Dairy Ltd
Gorwydd Farm, Llanddewi Brefi, Tregaron, Ceredigion SY25 6NY
Contact: Maugan Trethowan
Tel: 01570 493516
Product: Gorwydd Caerphilly Cheese.
Gorwydd Caerphilly has a delightfully full fresh taste, a firm creamy texture, and a natural rind which seals in the flavour.

### Silver
Neuadd Fach Baconry
Llandinham, Powys SY17 5AS
Tel: 01686 688734
Contact: Lynda Brown
Product: Dry Cured Bacon (unsmoked): back, streaky, middle, collar, and shoulder.

### Bronze
C & G Morgan & Son
Gellifeddgaer Farm, Blackmill, Bridgend CF35 6EN
Tel: 01443 672357
Contact: Gillian Morgan
Product: Own reared Welsh Lamb and pork.

**Bronze**
The Fruit Garden
Groesfaen Road, Peterston-Super-Ely, Vale of Glamorgan
CF5 6NE
Tel: 01446 760358
Contact: Lucy George
Product: Fresh Earth Ice Cream (8 varieties).

## True Taste Organic
The category for organic food and drink products.

### Gold
Bacheldre Watermill
Churchstoke, Montgomery,
Powys SY15 6TE
Tel: 01588 620489
Contact: Matt and Anne Scott
Product: Bacheldre Watermill. Organic Stoneground Flours
The best grain produces flour that retains the natural goodness of the wheat germ.

### Silver
Gellirhyd Farm Organic,
Llangenny, Crickhowell,
Powys NP8 1HF
Tel: 01873 810466
Contact: Mr and Mrs Gardiner
Product: Welsh Farmhouse. Organic Single Variety Apple Juice.

### Silver
Cambrian Organics Ltd
Horeb Business Park, Llandysul,
Ceredigion SA44 4JG
Tel: 01545 580680
Contact: William Lawrence
Product: Lamb burger with leeks and laverbread.

### Bronze
Rachel's Organic Dairy
Glanyrafon, Aberystwyth,
Ceredigion SY23 3JQ
Tel: 01970 625805
Contact: Jane Gosney
Product: Organic Low Fat Prune, Barley and Rye Yoghurt.

## True Taste Partnership
The category for products developed through collaborative production or marketing initiatives or joint ventures.

### Gold
The Welsh Whisky Company
Penderyn Distillery, Penderyn,
Rhondda Cynon Taff
CF44 0SX
Tel: 01685 813300
Contact: Edwina Clark
Product: Penderyn Single Malt Welsh Whisky.
The partnership between the The WWC and Brains Brewery utilises a brewing by-product to make whisky.

# True Taste/Gwir Flas
## Wales Food and Drink Awards 2004 – 5

**Silver**
The Welsh Meat Company
The Farmers Stores,
Newcastle Emlyn,
Carmarthenshire SA38 9DX
Tel: 01239 711506
Contact: Nicola Raymond-Evans
Product: Celtic Pride Premium Welsh Beef.
Produced by four leading partners within the food chain – The WMC, Wynnstay Plc, TH Sutcliffe Ltd & Castell Howell Foods Ltd.

**Bronze**
Gemelli Desserts
42 Bridge Street, Newport
NP20 4BH
Tel: 01633 251331
Contact: Pasqualle Cinnoti
Product: Torta Ricotta.
Produced in alliance with renowned Italian Patisserie, Lombardi of Italy.

## True Taste Manufacturer
The category for processed and speciality foods, manufacturers products and meals. This category has been split into small, medium and large based on a combination of factors from employment, turnover, distribution to production techniques.

## Small businesses

**Gold**
The Fresh Pasta Company
Units 5/6 Lon Parcwr Business Park, Ruthin, Denbighshire
LL15 1NJ
Tel: 01824 548119
Contact: Mark Garcia-Oliver
Product: Butternut Squash and Sage Tortelli.
Made from the finest 00grade flour and free-range eggs.

**Gold**
RK Palfrey of Newport
36a Church Road, Newport
NP19 7EL
Tel: 01633 259385
Contact: Peter Molesworth
Product: Welsh Salt Marsh Lamb Selection.
The company combines the old-fashioned good service of a traditional high-street butcher's shop with innovative meal solutions.

**Silver**
Mirandas Preserves
Tyr Henner, Goodwick,
Pembrokeshire SA64 0JB
Tel: 01348 872011
Contact: Miranda James
Product: Lemon Curd.

**Silver**
Cegin Suzanne
Penlanlas Fruit Farm & Golf

Course, Aberystwyth SY23 4QE
Tel: 01970 625319
Contact: Suzanne Lloyd
Product: Cegin Suzanne.
Preserves (Jams).

**Bronze**
Black Mountains Smokery Ltd
Leslie House, Elvicta Business
Park, Crickhowell, Powys
NP8 1DF
Tel: 01873 811566
Contact: Jonathan Carthew
Product: Smoked Duck Breast.

**Bronze**
William Lloyd Williams & Son
5 – 7 Maengwyn Street,
Machynlleth, Powys
DY20 8AA
Tel: 01654 702106
Contact: William Lloyd Williams
Product: Meats of the Seasons
– range of seasonal meats.

## Medium businesses

### Gold
Radnor Hills Ltd
Heartsease, Knighton, Powys
LD7 1LU
Tel: 01547 530220
Contact: Penny Butler
Product: Honest to Goodness.
Using entirely natural resources
of sparkling spring water and
pure fruit juices the result is a
contemporary and refreshing
drink.

**Silver**
The Patchwork Traditional
Food Company
Llys Parcwr, Ruthin,
Denbighshire LL15 1NJ
Tel: 01824 705832
Contact: Vicki Shenton-Morris
Product: Meat Pâté (3 varieties)
Lamb and leek, Pork and sage
with vermouth, and Pork and
laver bread.

**Bronze**
The Hurns Brewing Company
Unit 3 Alberto Road,
Century Park Valley Way,
Swansea Enterprise Park,
Swansea SA6 8RP
Tel: 01792 797321
Contact: Philip Parry
Product: Tomos Watkin OSB
premium bitter and
Tomos Watkin Cwrw Haf
summer ale.

## Large businesses

### Gold
Dairy Farmers of Britain
Blaydon Industrial Park,
Chainbridge Road, Blaydon,
Tyne & Wear NE21 5AB
Tel: 0161 827 5937
Contact: Sinead Robinson
Product: Cadog Luxury Welsh
Rice Pudding, Cadog Welsh
Butter and Cadog Vintage
Welsh Cheddar.

# True Taste/Gwir Flas
## Wales Food and Drink Awards 2004 – 5

Cadog Luxury Welsh Rice Pudding is the ultimate premium dessert. Cadog Welsh Butter and Cadog Vintage Welsh Cheddar is made using recipes unique to the Llangadog Creamery.

**Silver**
The Burger Manufacturing Company Ltd
Unit 1, Nyeside Enterprise Park, Builth Wells, Powys LD2 3UA
Tel: 01982 551713
Contact: John Hickin
Product: Kobe Steakburger.

**Bronze**
Serious Food/Sunjuice
Sun House, Llantrisant Business Park, Llantrisant, Pontyclun, Rhondda Cynon Taff
CF72 8LF
Tel: 01443 23722
Contact: Josephine Apperley
Product: Sunjuice – Raspberry & Boysenberry Fruit Smoothie.

## True Taste Own Label
The category for products produced under contract for other manufacturers or retailers.

**Winner**
Rachel's Organic Dairy
Glanyrafon, Aberystwyth, Ceredigion SY23 3JQ
Tel: 01970 625805
Contact: Jane Gosney
Product: Sainsbury's Wholemilk Natural Yoghurt.
A delicious, natural wholemilk yoghurt, produced exclusively for Sainsbury's supermarkets.

## True Taste Retailer
Open to all independent retailers, retailer operations and business including specialist retailers, e.g. independent butchers, bakers, delicatessens, farmers' markets, farm shops, box schemes, internet retailers.

**Gold**
Thyme Out Delicatessen
5 Elm Grove, Dinas Powys, Vale of Glamorgan CF64 4AA
Tel: 029 2051 2200
Contact: Rachel & David Lewis
Product: Delicatessen.
Welsh, local and organic are the key themes of this Dinas Powys delicatessen.

**Silver**
Edwards of Conwy
18 High Street, Conwy LL32 8DE
Tel: 01492 592443
Contact: Ieuan Edwards
Product: Butcher's Shop.

**Bronze**
Llwynhelyg Farm Shop

Llwynhelyg, Sarnau,
Llandysul, Ceredigion SA44 6QU
Tel: 01239 811079
Contact: Jenny Davies
Product: Farm Shop.

**Bronze**
Riverside Community Market Association
South Riverside Community Development Centre,
Brunel Street, Cardiff CF11 6ES
Tel: 029 2019 0036
Contact: Kenneth Moon
Product: Real Food Market. The Market is open every Sunday between 10am and 2pm. Venue details available www.riversidemarket.org.uk

## True Taste Hospitality
This category is bought to you in association with Wales Tourist Board.

## Caterer of the Year
Capital Cuisine
Unit 7, Tyndal Street Industrial Estate, Cardiff CF10 4BG
Tel: 029 2046 4090
Contact: Colin Gray
Product: Catering services. Capital Cuisine specialise in providing a high class, bespoke outside catering service which focuses on top quality food and impeccable service.

## Dining out
Dining out winners have been taken from the accredited restaurants appearing in this guide, see entry pages 30 – 179 for details.

### Best Newcomer
This award recognises a restaurant that has opened in the 2 years prior to publication of the guide and has gained an entry in Dining out in Wales for the first time and shows great potential.
**Winner** 698 page 128

### Best Use of Local Produce
This award recognises a restaurant that through its menu demonstrates an outstanding commitment to using the best of local produce.
**Winner** Carlton House page 120

### Best Restaurant of the Year
This award recognises an establishment that in the opinion of the judges has made an outstanding contribution to Dining out in Wales.
**Winner** Felin Fach Griffin page 51

# Harbourmaster

**The Quay, Aberaeron,
Ceredigion SA46 0BA
Tel: 01545 570755
Email: info@harbour-master.com
www.harbour-master.com**
On the harbour lane, follow signs for tourist information office

True Taste hospitality Bronze 2002-3

Aberaeron with its brightly painted houses and boats in the harbour, has always been amongst the most appealing of fishing towns. That said, the arrival of the Harbourmaster has done much to enhance its charm. Perched right at the end of the quay and easily recognisable from a distance as one descends into the town, the bright blue Harbourmaster stands as a beacon for the best of modern Welsh hospitality. Make no mistake, this is a fun place to be, relaxed in style and service with the food also having an easygoing unfussy style to it. The latter might typically comprise punchy starters of Welsh pork patties or squid and cockles deep fried with tartare sauce or mains of a wonderfully rich fish pie or lemon sole, perfectly cooked and served simply with good new potatoes and fresh green beans. Naturally, fish is often the best option here and they have the sense not to mess about with it too much. Service is cheerful, generally prompt and delivered by staff who seem to genuinely like working there, which always helps. A neat wine list offers plenty of good value and enough good crisp whites to accompany all that fish.

Owners: Glyn & Menna Heulyn  Chef: Sara Griffiths
Open: L Tues – Sun 12.00 – 2.00 D Mon – Sat 6.30 – 9.00
Closed: 24th Dec 2004 – 11th Jan 2005  Seats: 40  L £23 D £25

Visa/Mastercard/Switch/Delta  Map reference  **1**

**Uwchmynydd, Aberdaron,
Gwynedd LL53 8BY
Tel: 01758 760216**
Follow Brown & White signs to
Uwchmynydd from Aberdaron village

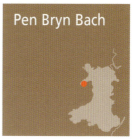

'Jolly' and 'unpretentious' sum up the feel of Roger Jones's long-standing and double dining room (and tiny lounge) where the décor is nautical and the repertoire stays consistent to please the regulars. What is on offer is a blend of Anglo-French dishes, with occasional forays into the Mediterranean and Asia. Fish is Roger's first love, not surprisingly given the location, with local resources including Aberdaron crab, Bardsey lobster, mackerel, sea bass and Caws Llyn cheese. Alcohol is a favourite saucing ingredient as in a creamy dry vermouth and herb sauce accompanying lemon sole stuffed with crab and scallop mousse, or the rich wine and cheese sauce of a seafood mornay. Devilled whitebait, shell-on prawns with mayonnaise and prawn cocktail are alive and well. There's smoked haddock chowder, as well as swordfish steak marinated in olive oil, garlic, garden herbs, tomatoes, onions and peppers, whilst hotpot of garlic mushrooms, goats' cheese filo pastry tart with caramelised onions, and chicken curry with turmeric rice offer non-fishy alternatives. There's a children's menu too. Home-made desserts like summer fruit crumble are good. Service led by Sheila Williams is cheerful and fairly priced wines suit the circumstances.

Owners: Roger & Jenny Jones  Chef: Nia Garner  Open: D only Tues – Sat (Bank Holidays & Sundays in main season) 7.00 – 9.00 Closed: 1st Oct – 1st Apr  Seats: 40  D £18.50

8 SC  P  V  Visa/Mastercard  Map reference

## Aberdulais

### Dulais Rock

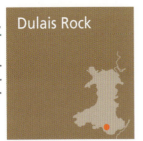

Main Road, Aberdulais,
Neath SA10 8EY
Tel: 01639 644611
Email: dulaisrock@tiscali.co.uk
www.dulaisrock.co.uk
Junction 43 of M4, onto A465 (Neath),
2nd exit, follow signs for Aberdulais Falls

Dulais Falls has been attracting visitors for many years since it became a National Trust property renowned for the drama and beauty of the watercourse and the richness of its industrial history. The neighbouring Dulais Rock is an inn with a colourful past of its own but its most recent incarnation is as a stylishly refurbished pub/restaurant with rooms and it has quickly become a destination in itself for those in search of good food in convivial surroundings. It's an all day operation with a panini style café menu throughout, a shortish light lunch menu and a longer, more ambitious menu for the evenings. The latter has a distinctly Italian accent and it offers dishes that have the full-flavours and generosity that distinguish regional Italian cooking. There's more than a nod to the locality though with local salmon featuring in a mousse with lemon dressing and home dried tomatoes as a starter or a main-course of Swansea Bay sea bass served with a crisp rösti and a Provençal tomato sauce. There is evidence of real skill in the kitchen with classics like gnocchi, risotti and panacotta all handled well. The wine list is relatively brief but offers plenty of interest and some very fair prices.

Owner: John Peace Chef: Nino Muccitelli Open: L all week 12.00 – 7.00 D Tues – Sat 7.00 – 9.30 Closed: Christmas Day/Boxing Day Seats: 50 L £15 D £20
20  3
Visa/Mastercard/Amex/Diners/Switch/Delta  Map reference 3

**Terrace Road, Aberdyfi,
Gwynedd LL35 0LT
Tel: 01654 767215
Email: info@penheligarms.com
www.penheligarms.com**
A493, coastal road from Machynlleth

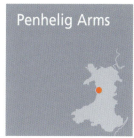

It began as a modest harbourside pub, but Robert and Sally Hughes's immaculate and much-loved hostelry has taken on board the virtues of genuine personal hospitality, simple, modern brasserie-style cooking and a dedication to fine wines (30 by the glass). Add wonderful views across the Dyfi estuary and stylish accommodation and you have the classic all-round inn. The very popular Fisherman's Bar has a traditional feel yet serves superior bar food to loyal locals and lucky visitors. With colourful modern paintings on the walls, the relaxed and unstuffy restaurant presents a daily changing lunch and set dinner menu. Expect simple, clean, fresh food with local fish and seafood the real highlight, although Welsh Black beef and local lamb do feature well. Mullet grilled with chilli, ginger and garlic and beautifully fresh tasting dressed crab are typical starters. Modern touches are evident in roast cod with lemongrass and star anise sauce and monkfish with roast peppers, pancetta and sun-dried tomato pesto, whilst simply grilled sea bass with paprika, sweet pepper and lemon is a real star, oozing flavour and freshness. Puddings may include caramelised lemon and lime tart with coconut ice cream or a plate of farmhouse cheeses.

Owners: Robert & Sally Hughes Chefs: Bronwen Shaw & Jason Griffiths Open: all week L 12.00 – 2.15 D 7.00 – 9.30 Closed: Christmas Day/Boxing Day Seats: 42 L £18 D £27

22  15

Visa/Mastercard/Switch/Delta  Map reference

# Abergavenny

## Angel

15 Cross Street, Abergavenny NP7 5EN
Tel: 01873 857121
Email: mail@angelhotelabergavenny.com
www.angelhotelabergavenny.com
Located in the main street of Abergavenny town centre

This historic coaching inn is a landmark in Abergavenny yet for many years suffered from a lack of real care under the ownership of a succession of chain hotel groups. Happily that has all now changed and the Angel is under local stewardship with a programme of refurbishment already underway. Owner William Griffiths is a man with a background in some of the country's best restaurants and good food is now at the heart of the hotel's attractions. The summer months find the attractive courtyard area packed with those lured by the brasserie style menu served there and in the bar. This is bright modern cooking with a blast of Mediterranean sunshine, and the 'Continental selection' a huge wooden dish of breads, meats, shellfish and marinated vegetables is terrific fun and great value. The more formal restaurant dining room (which is shortly in line for a makeover) offers cooking in the same spirit but a little more attention to detail. Dishes like pork and pancetta ravioli with smoked bacon sauce, smoked haddock and lentil soup or a main course of lamb noisettes with caramelised chicory are sturdy and full-flavoured. The wine list is brief but very well selected and includes at least 6 bins available by the glass.

Owners: Caradog Hotels Ltd  Chef: Mark Turton  Open: all week
L 12.00 – 2.30  D 7.00 – 10.00  Closed: Christmas Day  Seats: 70
L £12.60  D £22
150  29
Visa/Mastercard/Amex/Switch/Delta   Map reference 5

**Clytha, Near Abergavenny**
**Monmouthshire NP7 9BW**
**Tel: 01873 840206**
Email: clythaarms@tiscali.co.uk
www.clytha-arms.com
3 miles from Raglan on Old Raglan road

The Canning family's former Dower house is a great example of what all country inns should aspire to. Great beers, old time bar-room games and a warm welcome are the attractions of the old-fashioned – in the best possible sense – taproom. Andrew Canning attracts an enthusiastic dining public to his comfortable restaurant and is ably assisted by daughter Sarah in the kitchen. Andrew's food is bold and full of character. He is as comfortable drawing inspiration from the heady flavours of the orient as he is preparing his best selling dish of faggots for the bar. Expect such treats as a simple cracked whole crab with the fragrant Thai flavours of lemongrass, chilli and lime leaves but be prepared to get stuck in with the crackers and pick. Stylish puddings can include a zesty passion fruit crème brûlée or a traditional treacle tart with freshly made custard. The wine list is carefully selected but it would be a mistake to miss out on the opportunity to sample one of the well kept beers and ciders. Beverley Canning looks after front of house and a team of cheerful staff ably assists her.

Owners: Andrew & Beverley Canning  Chef: Andrew Canning
Open: L Tues – Sun 12.30 – 2.30 D Tues – Sat 7.00 – 9.15
Closed: Christmas Day  Seats: 50   L £18.95  D £18.95
20  4
Visa/Mastercard/Amex/Diners/Switch/Delta  Map reference  6

## Abergavenny

### Llanwenarth

**Brecon Road, Abergavenny, Monmouthshire NP8 1EP**
**Tel: 01873 810550**
**Email: info@llanwenarthhotel.com**
**www.llanwenarthhotel.com**
From Abergavenny, take A40 towards Brecon, 2 miles from Abergavenny

This roadside hotel will no doubt be a familiar landmark to users of the A40 between Crickhowell and Abergavenny. There is though a good deal more to this place than meets the passing motorist's eye, with the other side of the building accommodating a bright and spacious dining room that makes the most of peerless views across the Usk to the Brecon Beacons. Llanwenarth is now under the same ownership as Newport's Junction 28 and with bright flavours and quality ingredients it's not difficult to detect a similarity in the cooking styles. The menus offer an extensive choice combining à la carte with daily specials and a limited choice lunch menu offers especially good value. Dishes can be as simple as a smoked duck salad or a lunch starter of stir-fried beef in a filo basket but whatever the level of complexity, it's apparent that real care goes into preparation and accurate cooking of sea bass (with truffled mash and pesto) and monkfish (with king prawn Thai red curry and coriander noodles) are evidence of a steady hand in the kitchen. The wine list includes a large selection in the sub £15 bracket.

Owners: R Wallace & J West  Chef: R Scrimgeour
Open: all week L 12.00 – 2.00 D 5.30 – 9.30  Closed: Boxing Day/New Years Day  Seats: 90  L £14.25 D £20

18

Visa/Mastercard/Amex/Switch/Delta  Map reference 7

**Llandewi Skirrid, Abergavenny,
Monmouthshire NP7 8AW
Tel: 01873 852797
Email: francesco@thewalnuttreeinn.com
www.thewalnuttreeinn.com**
3 miles from Abergavenny, on the
B4521 towards Skenfrith

Walnut Tree Inn

Abergavenny

Francesco Mattioli took a brave decision when he decided to uproot from London and to end his career in some of the city's most famous restaurants to relocate in rural Monmouthshire. When that decision also involved purchasing a legendary restaurant from owners who had made it theirs for around three decades, one can only admire his determination. Rest assured, the Walnut Tree is in safe hands and ingredient driven Italian cuisine is still very much the order of the day here. A few tweaks to comfort levels have upped the ante front of house, but the main attraction continues to be the prospect of carefully constructed comfort dishes like the classic vincisgrassi or Anna's lasagne bolognese. Satisfying main courses might include tender middle white pork roasted and served with peas, broad beans and confit potatoes or deeply flavoured roast rump of Welsh Lamb with caponata, feta cheese and cherry tomatoes. Diners should be sure to leave room for the likes of tiramisu or home-made ice creams and sorbets – perhaps wimberry or fior di latte. The wine list is the work of a man with his finger on the pulse and offers excellent drinking at prices considerably lower than London's west end.

Owners: Francesco Mattioli Chef: Spencer Ralph Open: Tues – Sun
L 12.00 – 2.30 Tues – Sat D 7.00 – 9.30 Seats: 60  L £19.50 D £30
20-25
C Visa/Mastercard/Switch/Delta  Map reference

# Kinmel Arms

**The Village, St George,
Near Abergele LL22 9BP
Tel: 01745 832207
Email: tim@watzat.co.uk
www.thekinmelarms.co.uk**
Heading west, on A55 take junction for St George, heading east, take Abergele junction

Just south of the A55 expressway, the Kinmel Arms is a former coaching house on the edge of the historic Kinmel Estate and is said to date from the 17th century. The interior, grander than a country pub, with polished wood floors, deep sofas and tasteful décor, is divided between a traditional bar, a sunny conservatory and cosy, low-ceilinged dining rooms. Arrive early as the place bustles with eager gourmets. The attraction is the extensive, seasonally changing menu which features market fresh fish, local meats, fresh vegetables and Snowdonia cheeses. Chef Weston Holmes, cooks Welsh lambs' liver in a rich Guinness and mushroom jus and roast loin of local pork is stuffed with apples, apricots and herbs and served with a cream and pepper sauce. Fish fanciers will not be disappointed by chargrilled tuna steak served pink with a crisp Niçoise salad. Lighter lunchtime meals include sandwiches, mussels in a creamy white wine and dill sauce and fresh pasta dishes. Look to the chalkboard for inventive specials and home-made puddings like apricot puff pastry tart with crème anglaise.

Owners: Lynn Cunnah-Watson & Tim Watson  Chef: Weston Holmes
Open: Tues – Sun L 12.00 – 3.00 (5.30 Sun) Tues – Thur D 7 – 9.30
Fri – Sat D 6.30 – 9.30 (Also Bank Holidays) Seats: 88  L £16.95
D £16.95

Visa/Mastercard/Amex/Diners/Switch/Delta  Map reference

**Bwlch Tocyn, Abersoch,
Gwynedd LL53 7BU
Tel: 01758 713303
Email: bookings@porthtocyn.fsnet.co.uk
www.porth-tocyn-hotel.co.uk**
2 miles south of Abersoch, through
Bwlch Tocyn

Occupying an enviable position overlooking Cardigan Bay with views of Snowdonia, Porth Tocyn is surrounded by beautiful gardens. The hotel, once miners' cottages, has been in the Fletcher-Brewer family for three generations. Inside, the log fires, oak beams and comfortable cottage furnishings contribute to the cosy atmosphere, along with the young friendly team overseen by a lively host. The restaurant benefits from the sea views and offers a daily changing set priced menu. The chef combines lots of flavours to create innovative dishes with a touch of the exotic; although, the menu states that all dishes can be served plain if required. Sautéed kidneys are served on a garlic croute with pancetta and onion confit and a thyme and redcurrant jus; sardines are soused with lime and oregano vinaigrette, little gem, pickled cherry tomatoes, chorizo crisps and artichokes. Main courses include steamed mullet over rocket linguine with Provençale vegetables and sweet ginger and spring onion beurre blanc; and fillet of Welsh Beef with colcannon mash, Stilton ravioli, candied shallots and port jus. Puddings return to the traditional with crumbles, brulées and ice cream making an appearance.

Owners: Fletcher-Brewer Family Chefs: Louise Fletcher-Brewer & Douglas Hull Open: all week L 12.15 – 1.45 D 7.15 – 9.30 Closed: mid Nov – mid Mar Seats: 50 L £20.50 D £29.50

C  Visa/Mastercard/Switch  Map reference

# Conrah

Chancery, Aberystwyth, Ceredigion
SY23 4DF
Tel: 01970 617941
Email: enquiries@conrah.co.uk
www.conrah.co.uk
3.5 miles south of Aberystwyth, on A487

Dating back to 1753 though much changed by successive owners, Conrah has been in the hands of the Heading family since 1981. The house is an elegant retreat enjoying some spectacular views over the Cardigan countryside. The bright and airy restaurant is home to new chef David Carney's contemporary interpretation of classic French influenced cuisine. Expect competently handled versions of such dishes as French onion soup with a Gruyere crouton or pigeon breast with caramelised apple, black pudding and a raspberry syrup to start. Main courses often make use of great seafood from Cardigan Bay and this bounty may feature as grilled fillet of sea bass with sweet pepper and parmesan risotto or peppered loin of monkfish with smoked haddock brandade, sautéed asparagus, ratatouille and Madeira jus. Lunchtimes are more informal but modish favourites including a blackened tuna steak with punchy Caesar salad set the tone. Puddings often feature reworked classics such as an old fashioned pear 'belle helene' being updated for contemporary palates.
The wine list is compiled by Paul Heading who has a passion for things vinous and guests can expect some classic bottles at accessible prices.

Owners: FJ & P Heading & SL & JP Heading Chef: David Carney
Open: L all week 12.00 – 2.00 D all week, except Sun in low season 7.00 – 9.00 Closed: 1 week at Christmas Seats: 50 L £22 D £32

Visa/Mastercard/Amex/Diners/Switch/Delta  Map reference 11

**44-46 North Parade, Aberystwyth
Ceredigion SY23 2NF
Tel: 01970 612647**
Middle of town on one way system

After hanging up his fatigues, former Marine and Falkland's veteran, Harry Hughes trained as a chef, firstly at the Royal Naval Cookery School and later in some of London's finest restaurants. His cosy town centre hotel offers cuisine which exceeds expectations given the simple styling of the restaurant with its framed menus and comfortable chocolate brown leather chairs. With chef Chris Williams at the helm the cooking steers a steady course through the range of brasserie classics on offer. Gutsy starters may include rich rillettes of pork and rabbit with punchy piccalilli or perhaps goats' cheese and walnut ravioli with a refreshing sauce vierge. Main courses may include simply seared calf's liver with bacon, creamy mash and a red wine reduction or a more daring roast breast of chicken with a spicy tikka masala sauce. Puddings are well handled and may include a wobbly, orange scented bread and butter pudding. There's little ceremony to service and staff are enthusiastic and helpful. The short wine list is good value for money and a useful selection is available by the glass.

Owners: Harry Hughes & Li Harding  Chef: Chris Williams
Open: all week L 12.00 – 1.45 D 6.00 – 9.30 Closed: Christmas Day
Seats: 100  L £8 D £19.50
⋮⋮⋮ 40  ⇌22  P  ♿  V  🍴  ♣  ✕  ✂
C  Visa/Mastercard/Switch/Delta  Map reference

# Old Point House

**Angle, Near Pembroke,
Pembrokeshire SA71 5AS
Tel: 01646 641205**

Follow signs for Angle, then follow signs for pub and Lifeboat, down the lane and cross beach to pub

A favourite stop off point for walkers on the coastal path, the Old Point House is as close to the water as you'll find any pub in Wales. If you haven't enjoyed a walk before your meal, you may feel obliged to take one afterwards because this is hearty, enjoyable cooking that comes in trencherman quantities. The place is often bustling with happy locals and visitors alike. The best advice is to go for the specials board which comprises a wonderful array of mostly fish dishes that might include a smoked fish chowder as generous in quantity as it is in flavour. There is some imagination in the cooking with dishes like hake served with a creamy laverbread and cockle sauce or mackerel with rhubarb. The style is appropriately rustic but importantly, the cooking of fish in particular is accurate. There's plenty for the meat eaters too but it's really a sin not to do justice to such a selection of bounty from the ocean in this location. Puddings like jam roly-poly tend be equally homely and generous. A brief wine list is available but somehow a pint of bitter seems more appropriate.

Owners: Douglas Phillip Smith Chef: Lee Smith Open: (April – Oct) all week L 12.00 – 2.25 D 6.30 – 8.50 Closed: Tues from Nov – Mar
Seats: 50 L £19 D £19

50 3

C Visa/Mastercard/Switch/Delta  Map reference  13

**Panorama Road, Barmouth,
Gwynedd LL42 1DQ
Tel: 01341 280550
Email: enquiries@baeabermaw.com
www.baeabermaw.com**
From Dolgellau take A469 through Barmouth, 1/2 mile past clock tower, turn right and follow signs

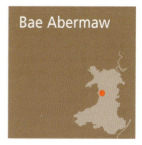

Bae Abermaw

Barmouth

Built of dark granite stone and impressively situated on a hill above Barmouth, with sweeping views over the harbour and out to sea, Bae Abermaw looks every inch the traditional resort hotel. Step inside and you'll be surprised to find a bold, strikingly modern hotel, handsomely refurbished in a trendy, minimalistic style, with white being the dominant colour and modern art adorning the walls. The contemporary blue and white dining room offers an adventurous carte that utilises Welsh Black beef, local salt marsh lamb and locally landed fish. Follow freshly baked bread rolls with a starter of plump scallops and tiger prawns, pan-fried with a mango chutney glaze and fresh herbs, or smoked swordfish with cucumber in saffron oil. Slow-roasted lamb comes with pease pudding and pickled red cabbage jus, while fresh and juicy sea bass fillets are served on laverbread tartlets with a pink grapefruit and cockle salsa and a sweet pea flower for garnish. Desserts might include baked blueberry cheesecake with blueberry purée, and banana and ginger parkin sponge with lemon toffee curd.

Owners: Richard & Connie Drinkwater
Open: Tues – Sun D 7.00 – 9.00 Seats: 26 D £28

80  14  P  V

C  Visa/Mastercard/Amex/Switch/Delta  Map reference

# Egerton Grey

*Barry*

**Porthkerry, Barry, Cardiff CF62 3BZ**
**Tel: 01446 711666**
**Email: info@egertongrey.co.uk**
**www.egertongrey.co.uk**
Off the Rhoose road, 1/2 mile from Cardiff Wales Airport

This old rectory epitomises the country house experience with its comfortable, cosy lounges and the elegant dining room which features magnificent, Cuban mahogany panelling. Expect to start with a surprise amuse bouche, perhaps a velvety smooth celery soup served in a demi tasse. Rob's cuisine capably combines the traditional with the more contemporary and the simple with the more technically complicated. Starters can be as straightforward as tender grilled squid with chilli and a lemony dressing or as impressive as scallop with black pudding, quails egg and confit tomato. Classic main courses such as roasted fillet of Aberdeen Angus beef with goose fat roasted potatoes, roast shallot, mushrooms and garlic vie for attention with contemporary ideas such as a Marco Pierre White inspired tagliatelle of oysters and caviar. Puddings see all the stops pulled out and few could fail to be impressed by an assiette of chocolate which features six different treatments of everyone's favourite ingredient. The wine list offers a super range of quality bottles which are keenly priced.

Owners: Richard Morgan-Price & Huw Thomas  Chef: Katie Mitchell
Open: L Tues – Sun 12.00 – 2.00 D all week 6.30 – 9.00
Seats: 40  L £19  D £30
16/40  10
Visa/Mastercard/Amex/Switch/Delta  Map reference 15

**Ye Olde Bulls Head Inn, Castle Street
Beaumaris LL58 8AP
Tel: 01248 810329
info@bullsheadinn.co.uk
www.bullsheadinn.co.uk**
On the main street, 100 yards from Beaumaris Castle

A stone's throw from Beaumaris Castle, the Grade II listed Bull dates back to 1472, though it was largely rebuilt in 1617. It shows its age well, the old timbered pub, hung with an impressive display of antique weaponry, is still the heart of the place and lively with locals. Step beyond and you'll find that the Old Bull has moved with the times as it's now a traditional pub, modern brasserie, stylish restaurant and smart hotel all rolled into one. Housed in the elegant conservatory extension, replete with heated Welsh slate floor, chunky oak tables and smart wine racks, the brasserie offers an informal atmosphere in which to enjoy good modern British food. No bookings are taken so the earlier you arrive the better, then order as much or as little as you wish from the large, eclectic menu. Snack on salmon and lemon mayonnaise sandwiches or linger longer over a starter of Thai chilli squid, then follow with roast whole sea bass with caramelised lemon, braised lamb Henry with onions and Guinness, or a first-class daily special, perhaps perfectly cooked tuna steak on bok choy with sesame oil dressing. Finish with a delicious baked vanilla cheesecake with fruit coulis. Brisk, polite and efficient service.

True Taste hospitality Gold 2003-4

Owners: David Robertson & Keith Rothwell  Chef: Steve Roberts
Open: L all week 12.00 – 2.00 D all week 6.00 – 9.00
Closed: Christmas Day/Boxing Day  Seats: 75  L £15 D £15

C  Visa/Mastercard/Amex/Switch/Delta  Map reference  16

## Ye Olde Bull's Head

**Castle Street, Beaumaris,
Anglesey LL58 8AP
Tel: 01248 810329
Email: infor@bullsheadinn.co.uk
www.bullsheadinn.co.uk**
On the main street 100 yards from Beaumaris Castle

Anglesey's flagship inn offers surprises at every turn. Regulars love the traditional bar for pints of ale and happy banter and the lively Brasserie for informal meals, but overnight guests and well informed locals book ahead for a real treat in the Bull's strikingly stylish upstairs restaurant. Décor is firmly up-to-the-minute with matting floor, purple high-backed dining chairs, big mirrors and bold paintwork. Keith Rothwell's contemporary cuisine keeps pace with the modern feel nicely. Key to the success is his knowledge of local suppliers and the kitchen's creative flair and confident handling, cooking and presentation of top-notch ingredients. Daily menus offer an imaginative choice at each course, perhaps a memorable crab terrine with saffron dressing to start, followed by tender, roasted rare venison medallions with sautéed wild mushrooms and delicious roast figs, their sweetness balancing the rich gamey juices. You could opt for roast Welsh Lamb with Conwy mustard sauce or sea bass with linguine and an orange and basil sauce. Finish with a refreshingly zesty lemon parfait. The encyclopaedic wine list has many treasures at easygoing prices.

Owners: David Robertson & Keith Rothwell Chef: Keith Rothwell
Open: D only Mon – Sat 7.00 – 9.30 Closed: Christmas Day/Boxing Day Seats: 45 D £33

⇌13 P V ⚐r ♣ ✕ ✤

C Visa/Mastercard/Amex/Switch/Delta   Map reference 17

**Bettws Newydd, Near Usk, Monmouthshire NP15 1JN**
**Tel: 01873 880701**
From M4 exit J24 to A449 Usk, follow B495 to Abergavenny

Black Bear

Bettws Newydd

This is the kind of place that makes you feel that you should really have earned your supper – either by prefacing it with a long walk or perhaps in pursuit of some of the game that features on the menu. There is no standing on ceremony here, the bar is understandably popular with local drinkers and although the restaurant area is tucked away, you still get the happy feeling that you're in a real country pub. The menu comprises a blackboard of enticing dishes with a real sense of the wild about them and might feature ultra-fresh crab (served with a sweet coriander dressing), fat scallops (simply tossed in garlic butter), partridge and mallard. The latter is a typically rustic dish cooked perfectly pink and served with a well-judged port and prune sauce. Portions are super-generous and you may find it hard to cope with a pudding but it would be wise to allow for it as the likes of an exemplary apple crumble shouldn't really be missed. A small wine list occupies another blackboard and there is always the option of a real ale or two.

Owners: Gill & Stephen Molyneux  Chef: Stephen Molyneux
Open: L Tues – Sun 12.00 – 2.00 D all week 6.00 – 9.30
Seats: 25  L £14.95 D £25
25  3
No credit cards  Map reference

## Tan-y-Foel

**Capel Garmon, Betws-y-Coed LL26 0RE**
**Tel: 01690 710507**
**Email: enquiries@tyfhotel.co.uk**
**www.tyfhotel.co.uk**
Off A470, towards Capel Garmon country house is on left hand side

The narrow winding drive up to this splendidly isolated 16th century farmhouse with its widescreen views over the Snowdonia National Park doesn't quite prepare you for what's to come. The Pitman family prove that urban loft dwellers don't have the monopoly on cool, modern interiors and the traditional rough stone exterior quickly gives way to fashionable tones of beige, brown and cream, contemporary lighting, art and furniture, plus plate-glass mirrors to make it all feel bigger. The daily changing dinner menu offers two choices until dessert and Janet Pitman's modern approach yields some interesting combinations characterised by high-quality ingredients and superb presentation. A willingness to play with flavour is a plus (as in a first course of organic chicken and thyme boudin with garlic bean purée and rich game jus) and combinations work – even a dish of roasted sea bass with spicy fishcake, shredded mange tout, tempura of broccoli and a dressing of olive oil, black treacle, chilli flakes and toasted sesame seeds. Delicate baked vanilla custard with apricot compote can end things well. Home-made bread is terrific, service from Kelly Pitman is first-rate and unassuming, and lively, modern wines come by the glass or bottle.

Owners: Mr & Mrs P K Pitman Chef: Janet Pitman Open: all week D only 7.30 – 8.15, booking essential Closed: Christmas/New Year and at times in Jan Seats: 12 D £39

Visa/Mastercard/Switch  Map reference 19

**Brechfa, Carmarthen SA32 7RA**
**Tel: 01267 202332**
**Email: info@wales-country-hotel.co.uk**
**www.wales-country-hotel.co.uk**
On B4310 in village of Brechfa

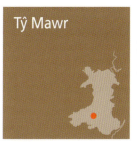

This lovely, atmospheric old house dates back to the 15th century and until 1970 was home to at least three families. The ground floor is a rabbit warren of rooms, full of stylish country charm: think bare brick, quarry tiles, antique rugs and wood burning stoves. It's a relaxed setting for a meal, with plenty of lounge and bar space for before and after dinner drinks. The menu pays tribute to Welsh greats such as Carmarthenshire dry cured ham (served with Brynmelyn beetroot chutney), lamb (served as a kebab on minted cous cous) and Welsh Black beef (with mushroom and pink peppercorn sauce). The straight talking cooking style admirably avoids messing with ingredients and shows a generally sound understanding of flavours – as in a tenderloin of pork with apricot and almond stuffing, its savoury flavours a good foil for a very sweet Cumberland sauce. The overall experience is highly enjoyable and is heightened by thoughtful little touches such as an explosively fruity raspberry sorbet to cleanse your palate before the main course. The helpfully annotated wine list travels the world but favours France.

Owners: Annabel Viney & Stephen Thomas  Chef: Stephen Thomas
Open: all week, booking essential  L 12.00 – 3.00  D 7.00 – 9.00
Seats: 30  L £16.50  D £27.50

Visa/Mastercard/Amex/Switch/Delta  Map reference  20

# Barn at Brynich

**Brynich, Brecon, Powys LD3 7SH**
**Tel: 01874 623480**
www.barn-restaurant.co.uk
East of Brecon on A470

Surely this is rural diversification at its most imaginative. Situated just to the east of the town, this complex – as well as being home to a successful restaurant – boasts an award winning caravan site, farm cottages and even a children's play centre. Whatever the associated facilities, the restaurant has plenty of appeal of its own. It's a cavernous building, simply decorated and furnished in a style that reflects the farming ancestry of the building. There are views across the sheep strewn countryside and the menu does its best to reflect what's good in the area, with Welsh Black beef bresaola, local duck and lamb all featuring on a summer menu. Choices are clearly aimed at serving a diverse market and range from sweet potato skins with cream cheese and chive dip or a chicken curry, to a generous 'jardinière' salad, chicken liver and foie gras parfait or organic salmon on a prawn bisque. Puddings might include a homely summer fruit crumble. Ingredients are well-chosen, flavours are generous but some dishes would benefit from a little more attention to detail. A short wine list offers a fairly prosaic selection but is reasonably priced.

Owners: C Maggs, C R, A M & M Jones  Chef: Andrew Addis-Fuller
Open: all week (Tues – Sun, Oct – Mar) L 12.00 – 2.30 D 6.00 – 9.30
Seats: 70  L £16 D £16
70  10 SC  P  V  r
Visa/Mastercard/Switch/Delta  Map reference **21**

**Felin Fach, Brecon, Powys LD3 0UB**
Tel: 01874 620111
Email: enquiries@eatdrinksleep.ltd.uk
www.eatdrinksleep.ltd.uk
3.5 miles north of Brecon on A470

The emergence of a rejuvenated Felin Fach Griffin on the eating out scene a few years ago was seen by many as welcome evidence that the revolution in pub dining was beginning to spread into Wales. The happy formula – unpretentious but high quality food, relaxed convivial surroundings and easygoing service – was something of an instant success with customers and guide books alike, but it is especially pleasing to see that far from inducing complacency, the early success has been built upon and that the food in particular is now arguably better then ever. The style remains no-nonsense; menus are sensibly short, descriptions to the point and there is an economical approach to the cooking that lets quality ingredients do the talking. It takes a skilled hand in the kitchen to pull this off though, and apparently simple dishes like rib-eye of local beef with chips and béarnaise or pork belly with leek colcannon and cider jus are distinguished by the precision of the cooking and fathom deep flavours. Much is made of local bounty such as Black Mountain smoked salmon and there's a welcome place on the menu for the likes of rabbit and woodpigeon too. Wines are well-chosen and the list is packed with interest and character.

True Taste hospitality 2004-5

Owners: Charles Inkin & Edmund Inkin Chef: Ricardo Van Ede Open: L Tues – Sun & Bank Holiday Mondays 12.30 – 2.30 D all week 7.00 – 9.30 Closed: Christmas Eve/Christmas Day Seats: 50 L £17 D £26

10-20 7

C Visa/Mastercard/Switch/Delta  Map reference **22**

## Tipple 'n' Tiffin

**Theatr Brycheiniog, Canal Wharf,
Brecon, Powys LD3 7EW
Tel: 01874 611866
Email: info@tipplentiffin.fsnet.co.uk**
Follow signs to Theatre and Canal

Whatever might be served up at the canal-side Theatr Brycheiniog, audiences can rely on one thing; if they do their pre-show dining in the neighbouring restaurant they'll find food that is a world away from the mediocre offerings that you often find at these kinds of venues. Although the exposed brickwork, light wood furnishings and paper napkins suggest a familiar formula, a glance at the menu indicates that something far more interesting is going on in the kitchen. Dispensing with the starter followed by main course protocol, on offer is a list of dishes that are designed to be shared as well as taken individually. It's a relaxed formula that extends to both the service and the style of cooking where the great strength is in the sourcing of ingredients. This is the kind of place where the leaves in a simple green salad can remind you of flavours you thought extinct. A similar commitment to quality is evident throughout the menu which may include Tamworth pork slow roasted with chilli noodles, organic salmon with pesto dressing, and rare strips of Welsh Black beef with the thinnest of fries. Prices are reasonable throughout and that includes the brief, but well-chosen wine list.

Owners: Louise & Richard Gudsell  Chef: Richard Gardner
Open: Mon – Sat L 12.00 – 2.30 D 7.00 (6.00 on shownight) – 9.00
Closed: Christmas Day/Boxing Day  Seats: 40  L £10 D £20

Visa/Mastercard/Amex/Diners/Switch/Delta  Map reference

**Coychurch, Bridgend CF35 6AF
Tel: 01656 860621
Email: hotel@coed-y-mwstwr.com
www.coed-y-mwstwr.com**
Junction 35 off M4, take A473
for Coychurch

Coed-y-Mwstwr

Bridgend

This charming red brick mansion was built in 1888, sits in 17 acres of woodland and these days is a smart country house style hotel with an associated golf course. Chef Chico Vidales offers a menu of updated classics with lavish dish descriptions that explain each offering in great detail. Expect starters such as scallops in a coriander and chilli marinade with black pudding fritters and herb butter or, more simply, smoked chicken liver parfait with salad leaves and melba toast to be competently handled and carefully presented. The occasional inaccuracy can creep in but largely the cooking is well conceived and based on good quality ingredients. Amongst the main-courses you can expect extravagant concoctions like peppered fillet of beef with Welsh honey mustard, tomato compote and mushroom stroganoff sauce, or a more simple lunchtime dish of salmon and asparagus with spring onion butter sauce. Puddings are something of a highlight with tasty, familiar constructions such as strawberries Romanoff or marbled chocolate terrine. Staff are charming and eager to please. An extensive wine list runs to 60 bins and includes the locally produced Glyndŵr.

Owner: Julian Hitchcock Chef: Chico Vidales Open: L Sun – Fri 12.00 – 2.00 D all week 7.00 – 10.00 Seats: 60
L £10.95 D £22.95
24 28
Visa/Mastercard/Amex/Diners/Switch/Delta Map reference 24

Bridgend

## Court Colman

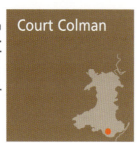

**Pen-y-Fai, Bridgend CF31 4NG
Tel: 01656 721122/720212
Email:
experience@court-colman-manor.com
www.court-colman-manor.com**
2 miles from junction 36, on M4, follow signs for Maesteg/Aberkenfig and then signs for Hotel/Gwesty

B

An unlikely setting for an Indian restaurant, this 200 year old manor house stands in six acres of landscaped grounds. The Bokhara Brasserie offers Indian and Mediterranean food, but it would be a shame to pass up the chance to eat food as it's done in India, which is a world away from your average curry house fare. The focal point of the restaurant is an open kitchen, flanked by phials of spices and though the décor is not as stylish as other parts of the hotel, its rich colours and subdued lighting make it an enjoyable setting. Knowledgeable, friendly staff are on hand to guide you through the menu and make it easy to order a whole spread of dishes – including a thick, flavoursome dal made by simmering black lentils and ginger garlic paste overnight over a slow fire. Flavours are clear and exciting, and as the kitchen eschews the common habit of using one base sauce for all dishes, each has a truly distinctive character. The Mediterranean menu includes sea bass baked in rock salt, oven roasted duck and chargrilled fillet of beef.

Owner: Vijay Bhagotra Chef: Vijay Bhagotra Open: L all week 12.00 – 2.30 D Mon – Sat 7.00 – 10.00 Seats: 90
L £10 D £13.95
250  30  P  &  V
C  Visa/Mastercard/Amex/Diners/Switch/Delta  Map reference  25

**High Street, Laleston, Bridgend CF32 0HP**
**Tel: 01656 657644**
Email:
enquiries@great-house-laleston.co.uk
www.great-house-laleston.co.uk

Great House

Bridgend

Norma and Stephen Bond's restoration of this former hunting lodge has been a labour of love conducted over many years. The building has been sympathetically restored and sensitively combines the contemporary with the historic. The mullion windowed dining room captures the mood perfectly with modish colours and table settings combined with period architectural features. Chef Neil Hughes offers a menu of modern classics with dishes such as potted rabbit confit or hot smoked salmon with summer beans proving accomplished starters. Main courses see great use made of quality local produce. Welsh Lamb features as perhaps a roast rump with savoury dumpling or as a carpaccio with port glazed beetroot. Lunch is an altogether more relaxed affair with dishes such as roast chicken Caesar salad or a comforting cassoulet of tomatoes and beans with three sausages. Puddings are well constructed but cheese lovers would be well advised to plump for the selection of fine Welsh cheeses with pear chutney and home-made bread. The wine list is carefully compiled and offers some excellent selections from France at good value prices. Terrific staff are attentive to their guests needs and always have a ready smile.

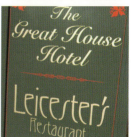

B

Owners: Norma & Stephen Bond Chef: Neil Hughes Open: L all week 12.00 – 2.00 D Mon – Sat 6.45 – 9.30 Closed: some Bank Holidays Seats: 85 |●| L £15.90 D £30

👥 70 🛏 16 🅿 ♿ Ⓥ 🚻 🍃 ✗ ♪ 🏛

C Visa/Mastercard/Amex/Diners/Switch/Delta  Map reference  26

**Near Broad Haven, Haverfordwest, Pembrokeshire SA62 3NE**
**Tel: 01437 781221**
**Email: jane@druidstone.co.uk**
**www.druidstone.co.uk**
2 miles north of Broadhaven, on coast road to Nolton Haven

There are few places in the hospitality trade that can legitimately be described as unique, but you would struggle to replicate the combination of characteristics to be found in this special hotel perched on the very western edge of Wales. In fact even the 'hotel' tag tells only part of the story - you'll also find cottages, a bar so popular that it's exclusive to residents and 'club members', vibrant support for music and the arts, together with a restaurant that has peerless views of Druidston Haven and the Atlantic beyond. Your first instinct might be that the place looks like it needs a good tidying up but you quickly get the feeling that there's just too much going on for there to be any point in doing so. It's not just the physical aspects that are remarkable, there is no standing on ceremony here and those that are wedded to slick, metropolitan service will do well to adjust to something much more organic. The food is similarly unfussy and lively, whether it be Thai style prawn kebabs featuring some fierce chillis, a more restrained but equally flavour-packed sea bass fillet with spring onions and vermouth or a faithful fruit-laden version of summer pudding. A good value wine list chosen with obvious enthusiasm adds to the allure.

Owners: Rod, Jane & Angus Bell Chef: Angus Bell Open: all week L 12.30 – 2.30 D Mon – Sat 7.30 – 9.30 Closed: Some dates in winter for refurbishment Seats: 35 L £16 D £25

12  11

Visa/Mastercard/Amex/Switch/Delta  Map reference **27**

**High Street, Caerleon,
Newport NP18 1AG
Tel: 01633 421241**
Follow signs for Caerleon, from junctions 25/26 M4

# Priory

## Caerleon

More baronial than bodega, this beautiful old building in the heart of Caerleon seems an unlikely setting for a thriving Spanish restaurant. Its dark labyrinth of ground floor rooms has leather sofas, reproduction oil paintings and a bar flanked by an impressive display of wine bottles. The restaurant itself is simply furnished with bare wooden tables. Modern Spanish music and plenty of slick, quick Spanish waiters are your first hint at the theme of the food. Order at the counter, which houses a tempting display of glistening fresh fish and generous cuts of meat. Behind it, a wall covered in blackboards lists a dizzying selection of dishes, from simply grilled kebabs, steaks or seafood through to daily specials such as a large, tender piece of venison in a punchy Armagnac and pepper sauce. Accompaniments include crisp, hand cut chips, new potatoes and an interesting selection of freshly prepared salads. Generally it all works very well, although there is sometimes room for greater attention to detail, in saucing and dressings for example. The wine selection is similarly expansive and contains some good value Spanish bins at the lower end of the price bracket.

Owner: Miguel Santiago Chef: Iain Jackson Open: L all week 12.00 – 2.30 (4.00 Sun) D Mon – Sat 7.00 – 11.00 Closed: Christmas Day/Boxing Day Seats: 130 L £13 D £27

40  22

C  Visa/Mastercard/Amex/Diners/Switch/Delta  Map reference 28

## Bryn Tyrch

*Capel Curig*

**Capel Curig, Betws-y-Coed LL24 0EL
Tel: 01690 720223
Email: info@bryntyrch-hotel.com
www.bryntyrch-hotel.co.uk**
On the A5, 5 miles from Betws-y-Coed

This unfussy and rustic building – part pub, part hotel – can be found five miles west of Betws-y-Coed in the heart of Snowdonia National Park. A blaze of summer colour outside, with the bar offering well-worn floorboards, comfortable sofas, basic tables and a big winter fire. The whole place is infused by a laid-back atmosphere which is matched by the friendly informality of the bar staff. A printed lunch menu is aimed at hungry walkers and less energetic folk out for a scenic drive, nothing more challenging than snacks of ham and local Welsh cheese panini, jacket potatoes, or Welsh rarebit made with Caerphilly cheese, mustard and local real ale, while the drill for dinner is a blackboard menu offering a good balance of meat, fish and vegetarian dishes. The repertoire is varied, weighing into shell-on prawns with garlic mayonnaise with a will and serving coconut and vegetable curry, or Vietnamese chicken and prawn hotpot, alongside grilled fillet of salmon with lime butter, or griddled chicken, with a choice of Stilton or devilled sauce. Puddings offer the comfort of sticky toffee pudding, lemon meringue pie, or bread and butter pudding. The modest wine list includes a few old favourites at fair prices.

Owner: Rita Davis  Chef: Phil Cousins  Open: L all week in peak season 12.00 – 3.00  D all week in peak season 6.00 – 9.00
Closed: Mon – Tues during Nov – Feb  Seats: 40  L £14  D £18

**C** Visa/Mastercard/Switch/Delta  Map reference  **29**

**97 – 99 Wyeverne Road,
Cathays, Cardiff CF24 4BG
Tel: 029 2038 2357
www.armlessdragon.co.uk**
Near Sherman Theatre

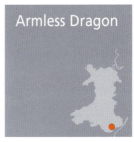

An unlikely location in a residential area close to Cardiff University, but it's well worth seeking out this striking and very contemporary restaurant to experience some really good modern Welsh cuisine. In fact, the culinary world would be a far better place if all city suburbs and big towns had a neighbourhood restaurant of this quality, one that is passionate about promoting the best local produce on short, well-balanced, seasonally influenced menus. Chef-proprietor Paul Lane flies the Welsh flag high above the capital, offering inspired 'Taste of Wales' tasting platters for starters. Opt for the 'Sea' and you could nibble satisfyingly on sewin pancakes, pickled John Dory and a delicious fishcake, preceded by a full flavoured crab soup. Main courses maintain the momentum, with sirloin of Welsh Black beef with mushrooms, roast tomatoes and onions, roast salt marsh lamb with greens, gratin potatoes and rosemary jus, and a beautifully fresh wild bass with baby fennel and a saffron cream sauce. Choosing a pudding is difficult with an impressive list may include bara brith bread and butter pudding and roasted figs with a rich balsamic syrup and cardamom ice cream. The 60-strong wine list typically includes two Welsh wines. Confident service.

True Taste
hospitality
Gold 2002-3

Owners: Paul Lane Chef: Paul Lane Open: L Tues – Fri 12.00 – 2.00
D Tues – Sat 7.00 – 9.00 Closed: 2 weeks Aug, 1 week Easter,
1 week Christmas Seats: 45 L £12 D £22

Visa/Mastercard/Amex/Diners/Switch/Delta  Map reference **30**

Cardiff

Bully's

**44 Cardiff Road, Llandaff,
Cardiff CF5 2DS
Tel: 029 2056 1996**
Situated at the rear of the
Maltsters Pub, Llandaff

Look for the Maltsters Arms, opposite the High Street in Llandaff, to locate Bully's in a converted stable beside the pub car park. Leased for the past seven years by the Bullimore family, this small, unassuming restaurant has seen its fortunes improve following the recent arrival of chef Tom Mansfield. With just seven tables it is advisable to book, the draw being Tom's seasonally changing blackboard carte and his bargain two course lunch menu. Ever-ebullient Russell Bullimore relishes his front-of-house role, enthusiastically describing each dish to diners, who learn that ingredients are locally sourced and that everything is prepared on the premises. For a quick, hearty lunch that won't break the bank, tuck into carrot and coriander soup or tomato and basil salad, followed by lamb's liver, mash and jus, or corned beef hash. Those with more time can linger over confit belly pork with roasted sweet potato, tomato and chilli jam and red wine syrup, then move on to rack of salt marsh lamb, perfectly cooked pink with a herb crust and served on honey glazed root vegetables and a rich garlic and lamb jus. To finish, try the refreshingly zesty lemon tart or opt for the plate of Welsh cheeses.

Owner: Paul Bullimore  Chef: Tom Mansfield  Open: Tues – Fri
L 12.00 – 2.00 Tues – Sat  D 7.00 – 9.30  Closed: 26th Dec for 2 weeks,
1 week end of May & Aug/Bank Holidays  Seats: 34  L £14  D £26

Visa/Mastercard/Switch  Map reference  **31**

**5 Romilly Crescent, Canton,
Cardiff CF11 9NP
Tel: 029 2022 1905
www.dacastaldo.com**
Off B4267 Llandaff Road

Da Castaldo

Cardiff

Many will remember these premises as being the home of Le Cassoulet for many years but these days this is very much the home of Italian rather than French cooking. Owner Antonio Castaldo is the man at the stove, and he has quickly established a reputation for good, fresh, Italian food served with real enthusiasm. A smart and modish room mixes blonde wood with light terracotta walls and blue seating. The food, though far away from the ersatz Italian cooking that used to be so prevalent, is comforting and generously flavoured in style, with the likes of polpette Napoletane (meatballs in fresh tomato and basil sauce) being both satisfying and excellent value as part of the lunchtime set menu. Many of the offerings are familiar and classic and may include a simple plate of prosciutto with fresh figs and mozzarella, bresaola, loin of pork with a Marsala sauce or classic saltimbocca a la Romana. Cheryl Castaldo leads relaxed and friendly service that is well-suited to the unfussy style of the food. The wine list offers a global selection but the emphasis, rightly, is on Italy and this is where the most interesting bins are to be found.

Owners: Antonio Castaldo & Cheryl Castaldo   Chef: Antonio Castaldo
Open: Tues – Sat L 12.00 – 2.00 D 7.00 – 10.00 (10.30 Sat)
Closed: Christmas Day & 4 days, 2 weeks in August   Seats: 45

L £13.50 D £24

Visa/Mastercard/Switch/Delta   Map reference

# Da Venditto

Cardiff

7 – 8 Park Place, Cardiff CF10 3DP
Tel: 029 2023 0781
Email: sherry@vendittogroup.co.uk
www.vendittogroup.co.uk
Opposite the New Theatre, in city centre

This stylish metropolitan restaurant specialises in the pared down cuisine based on great quality produce which is the hallmark of the new wave in Italian cookery. The sharp design is bright, contemporary and thoroughly suited to the modernity of the cooking and the city centre location. Expect such dishes as Spiedini of calamari and diver caught scallop skewered on a rosemary twig or wonderfully fresh beef carpaccio with rocket and parmesan salad to start with. Great risotti and pasta are, of course, always available and can be taken as starters, main courses or do as the Italians do and have them as a middle course. Main courses tend to be simple and to the point with great produce showcased in a straightforward manner. Free-range chicken could come with a punchy lemon and basil stuffing and some steamed potatoes. A delicious springtime dish of monkfish wrapped in top-notch pancetta comes with a carefully prepared vegetable casserole. Puddings tend to be delicately wrought versions of Mediterranean classics such as tiramisu or pannacotta. Be sure to take some time to study the thoughtfully composed – and almost exclusively Italian – wine list. Sommelier Paul Campbell is a real enthusiast and his advice is worth listening to.

Owner: Toni Venditto Chefs: Mark Freeman & Ifan Dunn
Open: Tues – Sat L 12.00 – 2.30 D 6.00 – 10.45 Closed: all Bank Holidays Seats: 55 L £17.50 D £32.50

Visa/Mastercard/Amex/Diners/Switch/Delta   Map reference 33

**Old Port Road, Culverhouse Cross, Cardiff CF5 6DN**
**Tel: 029 2067 0800**
Off the A4050

On the western edge of the city adjacent to the HTV studios, this is literally a great barn of a restaurant that has been successfully packing them in since the mid 90s. With its heavily patterned carpets and a dining area divided by wood railed partitions, it can bring to mind the chain restaurants that are to be found the length of the UK, but there the comparisons must abruptly end, because the great attraction of Gilby's is cooking that is light-years away from its more commercial counterparts. The kitchen is on full view from the restaurant and it is to his credit that more often than not it is the figure of chef/owner Anthony Armelin that can be seen overseeing the production of some seriously good dishes that range from superior versions of the familiar such as a traditional fish and chips – notable for terrific cod, light batter and great chips – to a precisely cooked starter of quail served with a Madeira and truffle jus. There is a sensitivity and care to the cooking that is especially welcome in the fish dishes and the waiting staff seem similarly committed to getting things right. Short, sensibly priced wine list with half-a-dozen by the glass.

Open: L Tues – Sun 12.00 – 2.30 D Tues – Sat 5.45 – 10.00
No details supplied
Map reference 34

# Holland House

**24 – 26 Newport Road, Cardiff CF24 0DD**
**Tel: 029 2043 5000**
**Email:**
**general.holland@macdonald-hotels.co.uk**
**www.macdonaldhotels.co.uk**
City end of Newport Road, 2 minutes from city centre

A recent addition to Cardiff, this 160 bed former office block, towers over the city centre end of Newport Road. It's an impressive conversion, stylish and with facilities that include a health club as well as the vast first floor restaurant and bar areas. The temptation must have been to locate the latter towards the top, where the views across the city are outstanding. Instead the visual distraction is provided by the open-plan kitchen where the chefs prepare well-executed versions of modern brasserie dishes. There's a lot of care taken in presentation with some showy crockery and fastidious arranging of items on the plate, but at root this is highly competent cooking. Starters like seared foie gras with pea purée, pressed duck terrine with kumquat pickle or mains like a classic rib eye steak or monkfish with onion risotto live up to their promise. Service is towards the formal end of things (to encounter white gloved waiting staff is something of a shock in itself these days) but consistently cheerful. A shortish wine list offers variable quality.

Owners: Macdonald Hotels  Chef: David Woodford  Open: all week
L 12.00 – 2.15  D 6.00 – 10.00  Seats: 145  L £18 D £23
2-500  165
Visa/Mastercard/Amex/Diners/Switch/Delta  Map reference 35

**Mermaid Quay, Cardiff Bay,
Cardiff CF10 5BW
Tel: 029 2049 2939
Email: info@izakaya-japanese-tavern.com
www.izakaya-japanese-tavern.com**
On the first floor of Mermaid Quay, overlooking the bay

An Izakaya is a Japanese tavern and this eponymously named restaurant captures perfectly the spirit of everyday Japanese dining. Iestyn and Yoshiko Evans have done an excellent job in creating this atmospheric addition to Cardiff's Mermaid Quay development. The stylish interior with its wooden beams, high bar counters and tatami matted rooms for private dining, mirrors as closely as possible an authentic rural Japanese tavern. Ordering a meal is a little unconventional for those used to a traditional three course meal structure – dishes arrive from the kitchen as soon as they are ready and a couple would need to order say 4 – 6 dishes to share. Classics such as tempura, sushi and sashimi are, of course, always available but some particularly interesting dishes such as Kawa Shioage, salted deep fried chicken skin – think superior pork scratchings – are certainly worth exploring. Great Japanese restaurants stand or fall on the freshness of their fish and guests can be assured that the Evans take great care to shop for the best possible seafood. Try the excellent mixed sashimi with grated Daikon giant radish. Wine is not best suited to this type of cuisine, do as the Japanese would and order an ice-cold Asahi beer or in colder weather a flask of warmed saké.

Owners: Yoshiko & Iestyn Evans Chef: Yoshiko Evans Open: all week L 12.00 – 14.00 D 6.00 – 10.30 Closed: Christmas Day/Boxing Day Seats: 90 🍴 L £14 D £21

👥 25

**C** Visa/Mastercard/Amex/Diners/Switch/Delta  Map reference **36**

# La Marina & El Puerto

*Cardiff*

**Custom House, Penarth Marina, Cardiff Bay, Cardiff CF64 1TT**
**Tel: 029 2070 5551 (El Puerto)**
**Tel: 029 2070 5544 (La Marina)**
On the marina overlooking the barrage

The Custom House – a majestic structure that dates from the mid 19th century – is an imposing landmark at the mouth of the rejuvenated Cardiff Bay. Such is the scale of the building that in its latest incarnation it manages to accommodate not one but two restaurants. Downstairs is El Puerto, yet another version of the order at the counter concept that has become so much a part of the eating out scene in this part of Wales. Here you can choose from lavish displays of fresh fish, meat and game that will arrive simply cooked and largely unadorned. If you're looking for something a little more sophisticated then climb the stairs to La Marina (no jeans allowed) where there is an à la carte menu presided over by Trefor Jones. Happily, the emphasis is still on simplicity, whether in a potent shellfish soup served with rouille, crawfish with lemon butter or venison with pepper sauce. The quality of the cooking demonstrates that there is a deft hand at work in the kitchen – all the more surprising then to find desserts that are largely bought in. The wine list offers plenty that's pocket friendly but also features some great vintages of classics like Lafite and Le Pin at second mortgage prices.

Owner: J.M.D Restaurants Ltd Chef: Trefor Jones
Open: La Marina Wed – Sun El Puerto all week L 12.00 – 2.30
D 7.00 – 11.00 Closed: Christmas Day/Boxing Day Seats: 500 total
L £12 D £18.50  150
Visa/Mastercard/Amex/Diners/Switch/Delta  Map reference 37

**6 – 10 Romilly Crescent, Canton,
Cardiff CF11 9NR
Tel: 029 2034 1264
Email: info@legallois-ycymro.com
www.legallois-ycymro.com**
Off the B4267 Llandaff Road

## Le Gallois – Y Cymro

At the epicentre of an expanding empire Le Gallois (a delicatessen and outside catering are now part of the package) continues to be a torchbearer for stylish cuisine in the Welsh capital. The buzzy atmosphere and crisp contemporary décor bring an air of metropolitan chic to this Cardiff suburb. Don't be fooled by the Francophile name; Chef Padrig Jones is unafraid to cast the net further afield for inspiration and is as at home with classics such as roast rump of Welsh salt marsh lamb with bubble and squeak as he is with modish dishes like an exemplary crispy chilli squid starter with a Napa 'Slaw (a Vietnamese style superior coleslaw without mayonnaise) and spiky chilli jam. Deftly wrought puddings may include modern classics like a sinfully wicked chocolate fondant with pistachio ice cream. Be sure to listen to your waiter's advice when choosing wine. A real strength at Le Gallois is the carefully chosen selection of about 15 wines by the glass and the front of house staff have a great understanding, pairing Padrig's food with an appropriate vintage. Understandably, France is most strongly represented and some delicious and unusual bargains are to be found in the French regional section.

True Taste
hospitality
Silver 2002-3

Owners: Jones & Dupuy Family Chef: Padrig Jones Open: Tues – Sat
L 12.00 – 2.30 D 6.30 – 10.30 Closed: 1 week Aug/Sept,
1 week Christmas & New Year Seats: 60 L £17.95 D £35

C Visa/Mastercard/Amex/Switch/Delta Map reference 38

# Old Post Office

**Greenwood Lane, St Fagans,
Cardiff CF5 6EL
Tel: 029 2056 5400
Email: christheoldpost@aol.com
www.old-post-office.com**
In St Fagans village

St Fagans has long been an attractive place to live, benefiting as it does from a pretty, semi-rural location but also being within a few minutes reach of the centre of Cardiff. For both residents and visitors alike this exemplary restaurant with rooms can only have added to the allure of the place. The restaurant is modish and carefully styled but manages to combine the contemporary look with real warmth, much of which is generated by an able and amiable front of house team. There is real attention to detail apparent in all aspects of the operation but nowhere more so than on the plate where the cooking has ambition backed up by genuine talent in the kitchen. An amuse bouche of pea and ham soup, bright, field-fresh and spiked with truffle oil is typical of cooking that has a lightness of touch but also real punch in the flavours. Perfectly cooked cod might arrive with a superbly-judged sauce vierge, chump of lamb with shallot purée and a wild mushroom and port jus. Desserts such as blackberry parfait with passion fruit sorbet and incidentals such as petits four are handled with similar dexterity. A great little wine list, packed with character, completes the happy picture.

Owners: Choice Produce Chef: Wesley Hammond
Open: L Thurs – Sun 12.00 – 2.00 D Wed – Sat 7.00 – 9.30
Seats: 28  L £15.95 D £32.50

Visa/Mastercard/Amex/Diners/Switch/Delta  Map reference **39**

**11 Kings Road, Canton, Cardiff CF11 9BZ**
**Tel: 029 2019 0265**
Email: info@patagonia-restaurant.co.uk
www.patagonia-restaurant.co.uk
From city centre, pass the castle on the right, over bridge, through 2nd traffic lights, bear right, 2nd left

There are times when life in a capital city can be, quite frankly, a little too frantic. Thank goodness, then, for havens like this. Calm, unhurried, relaxing; in direct contrast to the busy area it's in, Patagonia provides a welcome escape from the hustle and bustle of the outside world. Generally French-inspired cooking will feature ideas such as a marbled terrine of smoked chicken and confit of duck, crispy lamb sweetbreads or prawns and scallops with pink grapefruit dressing to start. Mains of corn-fed chicken with apricots or rack of lamb with Patagonian mushroom sauce are well conceived and presented, while the vegetarian choice is a good option, whether it's the starter of layered chargrilled vegetables with goats' cheese, rocket salad and tapenade or the main of home-made celeriac ravioli and truffle scented butter. The decadent rice pudding with coconut cream, pineapple and mango slices is a highlight of the dessert menu, as is the chocolate parfait flavoured with lavender. Unpasteurised French cheeses delivered every Thursday provide a heady footnote to a meal. The wine list consists of 20 decent bins, some available by the glass, for under £25.

Owners: Joaquin I Humaran Chef: Joaquin I Humaran Open: L Tues – Sat 11.00 – 2.45 D Tues – Sat 6.00 – 10.00 Closed: Bank Holidays & 24th Dec – 22nd Jan Seats: 42 🍽 L £12.90 D £25.90

36

C Visa/Mastercard/Switch/Delta  Map reference

Cardiff

## Tides

St Davids Hotel, Havannah Street,
Cardiff Bay CF10 5SD
Tel: 029 2031 3018
Email: tides@thestdavidshotel.com
www.roccofortehotels.com
Junction 33 off M4, follow signs for Techniquest

There can be little argument on the merits of the setting. Rocco Forte's stylish and minimalist hotel offers peerless views across the calm waters of Cardiff Bay and some of the best are to be had through the floor to ceiling windows of Tides restaurant. Some would argue that the food and service here have not always lived up to the surroundings, so it's encouraging to find that things seemed to have taken a step forward under chef Stephen Carter. The menu is long, strewn with classics and very enticing with a good range of fish and meat dishes supplemented by a string of simple grills. The challenge with a menu like this is to do the basic things well and by and large that target seems to be met. Carpaccio of beef, Caesar salad and foie gras terrine are well handled starters. Main courses like cod with chive mash and cockles or pork belly with savoy cabbage and a worcester reduction are full-flavoured and satisfying and desserts may include an excellent chocolate tart. None of this comes cheap and the best value is to be found on the lunchtime set price menu. The wine list has depth, plenty of character and is not short on extravagant options.

Owner: Sir Rocco Forte  Chef: Stephen Carter  Open: L all week 12.00 – 2.15  D all week 6.30 – 10.15  Seats: 100  L £17.50  D £35

C  Visa/Mastercard/Amex/Diners/Switch/Delta  Map reference   41

## Woods Brasserie

**The Pilotage Building, Stuart Street, Cardiff Bay, Cardiff CF10 5BW**
**Tel: 029 2049 2400**
**Email: gillesgeroni@aol.com**
Mermaid Quay, Cardiff Bay, opposite NCP car park

Whereas Woods once seemed to exist in near splendid isolation, these days it is surrounded by the myriad bars and eating places of Mermaid Quay. Nevertheless, this is a restaurant that still manages to stand out from the crowd. In part this can be accounted for by the Pilotage Building itself – listed, and the recipient of a sympathetic and striking makeover – but moreover it's the quality of the food that separates it from the majority of the pack. The set-up is broadly brasserie in style with sharp service from black-clad staff, bare tables crisply laid and food that is similarly unencumbered by fripperies. Typical of the style are a simple and well-timed seared tuna Niçoise (served like many dishes as a starter or a main), or a bright and fresh Mediterranean salad of roasted vegetables from the good value lunch menu. Key ingredients appear to be well-sourced if a really top-notch rib-eye steak (served with a straightforward and effective red wine sauce) is anything to go by and the quality extends to some competently handled desserts such as a jellied summer fruit terrine. The wine list has been chosen with some care with plenty of quality in the sub £20 bracket and there's a decent selection by the glass.

Owner: Choice Produce Ltd Chef: Sian Murphy Open: L all week 12.00 – 2.00 D Mon – Sat 7.00 – 10.00 Seats: 80-85 L £15.50 D £25
30-35
Visa/Mastercard/Amex/Diners/Switch/Delta Map reference 42

# Falcon

111 Lammas Street,
Carmarthen SA31 3AP
Tel: 01267 234959
Email:
reception@falconcarmarthen.co.uk
www.falconcarmarthen.co.uk

Situated in the centre of the market town, the Falcon has always worked hard on its food offering. It's the kind of hotel that has to serve a wide market, being popular with both business people and tourists, but deserves special credit for its commitment to serving fresh, tasty dishes with some emphasis on local produce. Chef Lubo Sorm offers an attractive, well structured menu in the bright, airy contemporary restaurant. Cockles from Penclawdd may appear in a fresh tasting gratin with spring onions or more simple pâtés and salads are typical starter dishes. Clean classical flavours are on display in main courses. Enjoy a carefully pot roasted breast of Guinea fowl with caramelised baby onions, bacon and a port wine jus or perhaps rump of Welsh Lamb with a redcurrant and raspberry sauce. Vegetables come as a generous selection served in communal style for everyone at the table to enjoy. Comforting puddings, perhaps bread and butter – taken upmarket with rich brioche – or a sinfully delicious sticky toffee pudding with ice cream are typical of the style. Staff are great fun and clearly enjoy entertaining their guests. The wine list offers around 50 bins and is keenly priced.

Owner: J R Exton  Chef: Lubomir Sorm  Open: L all week 12.00 – 2.15 D Mon – Sat 6.30 – 9.00  Closed: Boxing Day  Seats: 120
L £11  D £17.95
120  16  P

Visa/Mastercard/Amex/Diners/Switch/Delta  Map reference **43**

**2 Priory Street, Carmarthen,
Carmarthenshire SA31 1LS
Tel: 01267 238880
www.thymebistro.co.uk**
Adjacent to St Peters Church in Carmarthen

Thyme Bistro

Carmarthen

Situated on the edge of town this increasingly popular bistro has the pleasantly easygoing feel of a modern coffee bar. Wooden floor, large squashy leather sofas, low tables and the daily papers provide a relaxed area in which to peruse the menu or to just enjoy a drink. The menu is supplemented by blackboard specials and at lunchtime a range of open sandwiches are available as well as some simple pasta dishes for those wishing something lighter.
A new chef has arrived in the shape of Gavin Oram and he has put together a menu of bistro classics such as French onion soup, moules mariniere, seared salmon and steak with chips that are consistently full-flavoured and competently executed. Excellent roasted tomato soup is a good example of the style, bursting with flavour and finished with mozzarella and olive oil, while perfectly timed pork tenderloin is served on a green pea risotto with blue cheese and a rich sauce. Home-made breads such as olive focaccia are first class, puddings such as apricot and almond tart are not quite in the same league.

Owners: Mike, Kate, Paul & Tracey Kindred Chef: Gavin Oram
Open: L Fri – Sun 11.00 – 2.00 D Tues – Sat 5.00 – 9.00
Closed: Dec 24th – Jan 7th Seats: 70 🍽 L £15 D £23

 40

C Visa/Mastercard/Switch/Delta  Map reference

## Chepstow

### Wye Knot

**18a The Back, Riverbank
Chepstow NP16 5HH
Tel: 01291 622929**

Drive through town, Chepstow Castle on left, turn right at traffic lights, next left

As the name suggests this is a restaurant that benefits from one of those special locations – right on the banks of the Wye and shaded by mature willows. Inside where there is a small bar and a separate dining area, the atmosphere is cosy and welcoming with an abundance of foliage. Well-informed and outgoing staff offer enthusiastic advice on a menu that is not short on ambition and sometimes puts together some unfamiliar bedfellows. King prawns and excellent scallops for instance may come with sweet chargrilled Mediterranean vegetables and punchy dressings of pesto and balsamic vinaigrette but also a feta salad. The kitchen has the ability to do the classic things really well and seems at its best in this vein if a special of roast partridge breast with braised legs and a creamy smooth parsnip mash is anything to go by. Desserts are on the indulgent side with the likes of chocolate brioche pudding with peanut ice cream and butterscotch sauce being sinfully rich. The wine list offers a good range by the glass and a sensibly concise range of bins from across the world.

Owner: Emma Williams Chefs: Kevin Brookes & Emma Williams
Open: L Wed – Fri & Sun 12.30 – 2.30 D Wed – Sat 7.00 – 10.00
Closed: Boxing Day/New Years Day/Bank Holidays/2 weeks annual holiday Seats: 40 L £17.50 D £21.50 50 P

Visa/Mastercard/Switch/Delta Map reference 45

Church Bay, Near Holyhead,
Anglesey LL65 4EY
Tel: 01407 730241
Email: steff@coupe31.freeserve.co.uk
www.thelobsterpot.net
Junction 3, A55. Right at traffic lights,
then 6 miles to restaurant

Although owner Lindy Wood has leased her eponymous Lobster Pot out to long-serving chef Steffan Coupe she still makes her weekly trips around the Llŷn Peninsula to buy the best lobster and crabs for which the restaurant has been famous since the 1950s. Just a short stroll from the beach and memorable sunsets, this conglomeration of old whitewashed cottages has changed little over the years. Several dining areas with basic chairs and oak tables provide the simple setting for enjoying some wonderful fresh seafood. Naturally, lobster and crab come from the storage tanks next door, plump oysters are from the Menai Straits, while scallops and mussels come from the family's boats and Dover sole, bass and plaice are delivered to the door by local fishermen. Come in the evening for the best seafood choice (limited lunchtime menu), with lobster served every which way, sole simply grilled with butter, plump king scallops grilled with bacon, and beautifully dressed whole crab served with salad. Equally, carnivores will not be disappointed with roast duck, rack of Welsh Lamb with mint gravy and first-class steaks. Homely puddings take in bread and butter pudding and raspberry shortcake.

Owners: Steffan & Wendy Coupe Chef: Steffan Coupe Open: L Tues – Sat 12.00 – 1.30 D Tues – Sat 6.00 – 9.00 Closed: Christmas Eve – beginning of Feb Seats: 70 ¶⊙¶ L £12.15 D £20.25

C  Visa/Mastercard/Switch/Delta  Map reference

# Café Niçoise

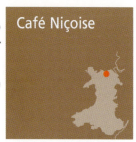

**124 Abergele Road, Colwyn Bay, Conwy LL29 7PS**
**Tel: 01492 531555**
**www.cafe-nicoise.co.uk**
Located on Colwyn Bay's main street, opposite Esso garage

This modern bistro of long standing saw a change of ownership in 2003 with Colin and Eileen Kershaw taking over, but the Gallic-inspired décor remains – wood floor, terracotta colours, close-packed white clothed tables – and the kitchen continues to serve dishes based on native ingredients and built around ideas from the Mediterranean. Grilled goats' cheese with a tomato and basil salad and yoghurt dressing and wild boar with sweet potato and apple purée are typical, while fish is fresh and generally well handled, producing a firm and succulent piece of wild sea bass with braised chicory and dill, for example. Welsh Lamb plays its part too, as do one or two trendier touches such as Orkney herrings marinated in a sweet Madeira sauce and asparagus and mint risotto. 'Ample portions' sums it all up, whether a hefty pressed chicken and leek terrine with a root vegetable chutney, or Scottish fillet of beef with fondant potatoes and sloe gin sauce. Desserts might take in caramelised pear flan with pear coulis, or summer fruit pudding tower with strawberry ice cream. Notable is solicitous service and the wine selection is a short, sound list with half-a-dozen by the glass from £2.80.

Owners: Colin & Eileen Kershaw  Chef: Chris Jackson
Open: L Wed – Sat 12.00 – 1.45  D Tues – Sat 7.00 – 9.45
Closed: 26th – 30th Dec  Seats: 26  L £18.10  D £18.10

26  P  V  r

Visa/Mastercard/Amex/Diners/Switch/Delta  Map reference 47

**Castle Hotel, High Street,
Conwy LL32 8DB
Tel: 01492 582800
Email: mail@castlewales.co.uk
www.castlewales.co.uk**
In the centre of Conwy

Congenial and comfortable is a fair description of this civilized red-brick Victorian hotel. Shakespeare's Restaurant – it boasts paintings of the bard's characters by the Victorian artist John Dawson-Watson – is plush without being unduly lavish and is beginning to attract a loyal following.

Graham Tinsley's culinary tone is very much in the country-house mould and there may be chicken liver parfait with a grape and sauternes compote and Melba toast to start, followed by fillet of turbot with boulangère potatoes, carrot purée and glazed baby leeks. Among livelier modern offerings, substantial first courses may run to a gutsy pan-seared black pudding and braised belly pork, soft poached hen's egg and creamy hollandaise sauce, while a main course duck breast is teamed with sticky red cabbage, potato terrine, pear chutney and sage and white bean jus. Rum baba with a compote of hedgerow berries is an imaginative dessert. The cooking doesn't aim to dazzle, but steers a steady course through the prime ingredients that constitute the foundation of the menu. The well-annotated wine list can be relied on to furnish a sound bottle at a reasonable price; house selections range from £11.75 to £15.75.

Owners: Castle Hotel Conwy Ltd Chef: Graham Tinsley Open: L Sun 12.30 – 2.30 D all week 7.00 – 9.30 Seats: 55 L £15 D £25

28

Visa/Mastercard/Amex/Switch/Delta  Map reference

# Huddarts

**69 High Street, Cowbridge**
**Vale of Glamorgan CF71 7AF**
**Tel: 01446 774645**
Situated on main High Street, opposite Barclays Bank

Husband and wife team Andrew and Julie Huddart's town centre restaurant attracts a loyal following. Andrew is a classically trained chef who produces accurate, well balanced meals and Julie is an engaging hostess who supervises the dining room. Their traditionally styled townhouse restaurant is restrained and calm in style and offers a very grown up dining experience with fine table linen and sparkling glassware to set the scene. Andrew makes great use of local bounty and is keen to detail the origins of his produce on the extensive, well constructed menu. The curtain raiser canapés help to stave off hunger pangs while choosing. Choose wisely and you may be in for a treat, perhaps being offered some super fresh langoustines, simply poached and served with a delicious garlic butter. A lamb main course (salt marsh when available) may come as roasted saddle on a bed of tender confit with an accurate, carefully reduced, red wine sauce. Puddings continue in the classic vein but who could resist an unctuous bread and butter pudding or perhaps crunchy pavlova with ripe berries and cream. The wine list is carefully constructed and house wines are very good value.

Owners: Julie & Andrew Huddart  Chef: Andrew Huddart
Open: L Tues – Sun 12.00 – 1.45  D Tues – Sat 7.00 – 9.15
Closed: First two weeks in Jan, 1 week in Spring, 1 week in Sept
Seats: 32  L £15.85  D £27.85
C  Visa/Mastercard/Switch/Delta  Map reference

**28 High Street, Cricceith, Gwynedd
LL52 0BT
Tel: 01766 522506**
On the main High Street in Cricceith

The restaurant is in a parade of shops and is comfortable and fastidiously furnished. In a seaside town like Cricceith it's smart thinking to offer a two-tiered eating and drinking operation, and Granvilles' does that with a café-style set-up during the day, delivering coffee and cakes, sandwiches, salads, plus a few main courses and puddings, then morphing into a restaurant in the evening with a full-blown à la carte. It works well, pulled together by on-the-ball service, a genuine welcome for families matched by a first-rate children's menu, and Colin Pritchard's varied and interesting repertoire. Subtle sauces, sound buying and touches of ambition are what impress and the kitchen shows its mettle with avocado and smoked chicken Caesar salad, baked Anglesey crab with lemon and watercress, simply grilled fillet of Cardigan Bay sea bass with chargrilled asparagus, lemon and herb mayonnaise and herb-crusted cutlets of lamb (served pink) with a leek risotto and rosemary and garlic potatoes. If you planned to skip dessert and instead head for the celebrated Cadwallader's ice cream shop, you're missing treats like an outstanding caramelised lemon tart with an intense blackcurrant sorbet or apricot crème brûlée. The short wine list is a reasonably priced global slate.

Owners: Colin & Delyth Pritchard Chef: Colin Owen Pritchard
Open: Thurs – Tues L 12.00 – 2.00 D 6.00 – 9.00
Closed: 17th Dec – 1st Mar Seats: 44 L snacks £5 – 8 D £22

Visa/Mastercard/Switch/Delta Map reference 50

# Bear

**Crickhowell, Powys NP8 1BW**
**Tel: 01873 810408**
**Email: bearhotel@aol.com**
**www.bearhotel.co.uk**
Centre of town

This Crickhowell institution has been delighting travellers for many generations and the Bear continues to be both a destination for pilgrims and also the hub of this charming town's social life. The convivial bars are very much the heart of the hotel operation with great beers, honest food and a genuine welcome afforded to all. Those seeking a more romantic meal are carefully looked after in the elegant candlelit dining room. Drawing on a wealth of influences from across the globe the chefs produce such dishes as hot and sour pickled prawns with peppers and limes or a pleasing vegetarian ricotta and spinach gnocchi with tomato and basil. Great Welsh ingredients including lamb and beef feature in main courses which range from the simple – T-bone steak with a choice of sauces – to the more ambitious scallops wrapped in bacon with sage and a sun-dried tomato sauce. Puddings are a real treat here and some do demand a trencherman's appetite – the house speciality of bread and butter pudding with rum, bananas and brown bread ice cream certainly demands commitment from diners. The wine list is well chosen and features a good range of vintages available by the glass or in half bottle format.

Owners: J Hindmarsh & Stephen Hindmarsh Chefs: Justin Howe & Brian Simmonds Open: L all week 12.00 – 2.00 (Bar only) D Tues – Sat 7.00 – 9.30 Closed: Residents only Christmas Day Seats: 60

D £25

Visa/Mastercard/Amex/Switch/Delta  Map reference 51

**Brecon Road, Crickhowell, Powys
NP8 1SG
Tel: 01873 810775
Email: info@cidermill.co.uk
www.cidermill.co.uk**
1 mile outside of Crickhowell, on A40, towards Brecon, at the junction of the A479

## Nantyffin Cider Mill Inn

Crickhowell

This pink washed old drovers inn on the banks of the River Usk remains a local institution with its intimate cosy dining rooms and outside tables for fine weather dining. Still upholding a tradition of great beers (and ciders) and honest, no nonsense fare which never fails to satisfy, Nantyffin is a great stop off on the A40. Fine organic meat is reared especially for the Inn (and its sister properties) at the owners farm in Llangyndir and this holistic approach to food and eating pays obvious rewards. Nantyffin has a great sense of 'place' about its offering, with beers, cider, meat and even whisky being sourced locally. Besides local producers, the other beneficiaries are other diners who can expect to enjoy satisfying dishes like confit of organic lamb with olive oil mash and a rosemary and garlic sauce. Rib eye of beef is frequently served straight from the chargrill with crisp hand cut chips, Portobello mushroom and oven roasted tomato, simple but supremely satisfying in these surroundings. Great staff who clearly love their work add to the experience and the wine list is an exemplary exercise in clarity and choice.

Owners: Glyn & Jessica Bridgeman & Sean Gerrard
Chef: Sean Gerrard Open: L Tues – Sun 12.00 – 2.30 D Tues – Sat 6.30 – 9.30 Closed: Christmas Day/Boxing Day Seats: 65

L £12.95 D £20

C Visa/Mastercard/Amex/Switch/Delta  Map reference

# Nant Ddu Lodge

**Cwm Taf, Near Merthyr Tydfil,
Powys CF48 2HY
Tel: 01685 379111
Email: enquiries@nant-ddu-lodge.co.uk
www.nant-ddu-lodge.co.uk**
On the A470, 6 miles north of Merthyr Tydfil and 12 miles south of Brecon

It is little more than a decade since the Ronson family took over a modest country hotel positioned between the top of the South Wales valleys and the Brecon Beacons. In the years since, they have wrought a remarkable transformation which has seen the award winning hotel double in size with the most recent addition being a smart new spa complex. Food has always been at the heart of matters with a traditional bar supplemented by a bright, contemporary looking bistro. Whatever venue you choose the menu is the same, although there is more in the way of formal service in the bistro. The style of cooking takes something of a global sweep with the likes of Cajun chicken with barbecue sauce keeping company with sardines, couscous and roasted tomato dressing or a simply poached fillet of sewin with a spinach cream sauce. The common thread is down-to-earth cooking that may not always be perfect, but is rarely short of generous flavours, especially in some satisfying desserts such as an indulgent gooseberry trifle. Main courses in particular are very fairly priced, as is a short wine list that nevertheless manages to cater for most tastes.

Owners: David Ronson Chef: Richard Wimmar Open: all week
L 12.00 – 2.30 D 6.30 – 9.30 Closed: Christmas Day/Boxing Day Eve
Seats: 120   L £22 D £22

20   32   P  &  V    ⚘  ✕  ≉  ⌂

C  Visa/Mastercard/Amex/Switch/Delta   Map reference  53

**Cwmdu, Crickhowell, Powys NP8 1RU**
Tel: 01874 730464
Email: cwmdu@aol.com
www.thefarmersarms.com

From Crickhowell, take A40 towards Brecon, after 1.5 miles take A479 (Builth Wells), then 3 miles to Cwmdu

Farmers Arms

Cwmdu

The food may be a big part of the attraction here but the Farmers Arms manages to pull off that special trick of being a good local as well as an eating destination. It's a combination that ensures there is often a bustle about the place both in the bar and the separate restaurant. It's great to find a place comfortable with a menu that can accommodate both a superior version of classic Welsh cawl and more cosmopolitan ideas like king prawn tempura or confit leg and pan-fried breast of duck with a Welsh honey and plum sauce. Portions are generous with the style being unfussy but benefiting from accurate cooking and some punchy flavours. Roast rack of 'Rhiangoll' lamb, nicely pink and accompanied by a sturdy brussel sprout mash is typical of the style and it's good to see the use of plenty of Welsh bounty such as Gower sea bass steamed in a foil packet with ginger spring onions and lime. Upbeat, cheerful service comes in an appropriately easygoing manner. Wines are of course available but the real attraction are some great cask conditioned ales.

Owners: Andrew & Susan Lawrence  Chefs: Andrew & Susan Lawrence
Open: L Wed – Sun 12.00 – 2.00 (2.30 Sun) D Tues – Sun 7.00 – 9.15 (9.30 Fri/Sat) Closed: 2 weeks Nov & Jan  Seats: 40  L £12 D £20

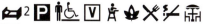

C Visa/Mastercard/Switch/Delta  Map reference  54

# Sands Bar and Brasserie

59 – 63 Station Road,
Deganwy LL31 9DF
Tel: 01492 592659
www.sandsbrasserie.com
Opposite Deganwy Castle Hotel,
in Deganwy

Clear plate glass, clean lines and lots of blonde wood mark out the modern interior of this restaurant set in a long parade of shops and small businesses opposite Deganwy railway station. Paul Taylor and Karen Cmela took over in early 2004 with a clear purpose and message. They aim to make good food widely available and achieve it with the help of sound ingredients, sensitive cooking and a fair pricing policy. At heart is a varied repertoire, equally at home with salt and pepper squid with Thai noodles, sweet chilli and mint, as with pan-fried lambs' kidneys with wild mushroom rice, green peppers and brandy cream and taking in marinated chicken on Moroccan couscous with mint yoghurt, or garden pea and asparagus risotto with basil and pine nuts, along the way. Behind all the cooking is a degree of skill that can knock up perfect lamb rump (cooked pink) with flageolet beans, sweet potato, beetroot and red wine to order and service that does all the right things. Desserts might include sparkling white wine fruit jelly with mascarpone, or a comforting peach and pear crumble with vanilla ice cream. Wines are a short, eclectic bunch, opening at £10.50 and struggling to get above £15.

Owners: Paul Taylor & Karen Cmela  Chef: Rob Parry  Open: Tues – Sat
L 12.00 – 2.30  D 6.00 – 9.30  Closed: 1st two weeks in Jan
Seats: 32  L £19  D £25  25
Visa/Mastercard/Amex/Diners/Switch/Delta  Map reference 55

**2 Ffos-y-Felin, Dolgellau,
Gwynedd LL40 1BS
Tel: 01341 422870
Email: dylan@dylanwad.co.uk
www.dylanwad.co.uk**
Centre of town, on the one-way system

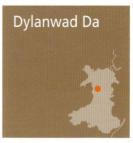

The wine-red façade of Dylan Rowland's informal and unfussy little bistro stands out against the granite-grey stone buildings in Dolgellau. By day it's a bustling coffee bar, whilst at night soft lighting and candlelight draw diners into the narrow dining room, kitted out with pine tables and high-backed chairs and modern art on the walls, for some eclectic bistro fare. Monthly menus are sensibly short and straightforward and Dylan makes good use of fresh local ingredients, in particular Welsh Lamb and beef. Simple starters may take in Dolgellau rarebit with plum chutney or thick slices of coarse pork and herb paté. Plentiful vegetables, perhaps a spicy ratatouille and crisp green beans, may accompany a tender and perfectly cooked sirloin of beef with a rich Danish blue and red wine sauce, a casserole of lamb, port, plum and ginger, or the single fish option on the menu, for example salmon fillet with prawn sauce. If you have room, round off with chocolate sponge tart, almond praline ice cream with toffee sauce, or a plate of Welsh cheese. Dylan runs a 'Dan y Dylanwad' wine business and the list offers plenty of interest, including some good value clarets. Efficient service from young, Welsh speaking staff.

Owner: Dylan Rowlands Chef: Dylan Rowlands Open: Tues – Sat (summer) Thurs – Sat (winter) D 7.00 – 9.00 Closed: February Seats: 28 🍴 D £22

 Map reference 56

## Erbistock

### Boat

**Erbistock, Wrexham LL13 0DL**
**Tel: 01978 7800666**
**Email: info@theboatinn.co.uk**
**www.theboatinn.co.uk**
In the village by River Dee

The Boat is not the easiest place to find but is well worth the journey; situated at the end of a no through road the pretty building sits alongside the River Dee, surrounded by beautiful countryside. Originally two separate cottages, they have now been joined together by a conservatory to extend the dining area, which along with the tables by the river, is a particularly pleasant venue for lunch. One end of the building houses a cosy bar and the other end the restaurant, an attractive blend of rustic cottage and modern bistro; a wooden floor and terracotta painted stone walls are given a contemporary twist with the marble topped wooden tables, and the cast iron and cane chairs. The menu changes seasonally with dishes such as Welsh Lamb shank and crushed new potatoes, smoked chicken Caesar salad or Boat Inn cod in beer batter with chips and mushy peas and there is always a home-made pie of the day. At lunchtime a range of sandwiches is also available, including open ciabatta sandwiches and tortilla wraps.

Owner: M Cooke Chef: Gareth Payne Open: all week L 12.00 – 2.30 D 6.30 9/9.30 Closed: Sun evenings (Oct – Mar) New Years Day
Seats: 84  L £16 D £24
48
Visa/Mastercard/Switch/Delta   Map reference **57**

**Y Llech, Harlech, Gwynedd LL46 2YL**
**Tel: 01766 780479**
**Email: glyn@castlecottageharlech.co.uk**
**www.castlecottageharlech.co.uk**
Small white building, just off high street, close to the castle

## Castle Cottage

*Harlech*

The core of this stone-built cottage close to Harlech Castle is old, with a cosily traditional bar and sitting room plus a dining room that's smart and trim. The Glyn and Jacqueline Roberts stamp is clearly seen, she in almost perpetual motion front of house serving food and drink, he in the kitchen deploying local ingredients and modern ideas. There may be no surprises on the menu, but that is not to say that it is dull. Carmarthen air-dried ham with grilled Turkish figs and Perl Las blue cheese makes a provocative starter, duck liver and Cointreau parfait with red onion marmalade and toasted brioche a homelier one. Saucing is effective (a beurre blanc sauce for a fillet of Milford Haven hake baked with herb and laverbread crust, for example) and although a certain richness is typical of the food – as in boned and rolled suckling pig with black pudding, red cabbage and Calvadois jus – good judgement ensures that the end result is not too heavy. Light desserts such as lemon posset, or brandy snap basket of summer berries with coconut ice cream are a welcome finish. Good choice and fair value distinguish the wine list.

**H**

Owners: Glyn & Jacqueline Roberts Chef: Glyn Roberts
Open: all week D 7.00 – 9.30 Closed: 3 weeks in January
Seats: 45 D £27.50 8
C Visa/Mastercard/Switch/Delta Map reference  58

# Maes-y-Neuadd

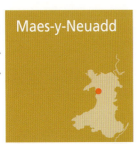

**Talsarnau, Near Harlech, Gwynedd LL47 6YA**
**Tel: 01766 780200**
**Email: maes@neuadd.com**
**www.neuadd.com**
3 miles north east of Harlech, follow brown signs

Peace and calm are among the attributes of this comfortable granite and slate house set in glorious isolation in the Snowdonia National Park, whilst thick walls, beams and low ceilings attest to its age. Since the famed walled vegetable gardens are stocked with an amazing variety of herbs, vegetables and fruits it would be surprising if a few of them didn't make it to the kitchen and indeed they crop up in herb sauces, honey-roasted vegetables, home-made chutneys and the like. Interesting ideas abound, from the pickled white cabbage and green peppercorn sauce that accompanies a lunchtime confit of duck, to the Brecon venison with haricot casserole plus garlic and raspberry coulis offered at dinner. Rillette of game or air-dried beef can open precedings, whilst desserts can be as comforting as bread and butter pudding with fresh egg custard, or as light as glazed blackberries with Grand Marnier sabayon. Different flavoured breads add interest, splendid service is a plus and the wide ranging, serious wine list combines variety and quality with good value for money, opening with a broad selection under £16.

Owners: Lynn & Peter Jackson, Peter & Doreen Payne
Chef: Peter Jackson Open: all week L 12.00 – 13.45 D 7.00 – 8.45
Seats: 65 L £12 D £31

12  16  P  r

Visa/Mastercard/Amex/Switch/Delta  Map reference  59

**24 Market Street, Haverfordwest,
Pembrokeshire SA61 1NH
Tel: 01437 766683
Email: llewis6140@aol.com**
Halfway down Market Street, near the Palace cinema

George's is full of surprises. The bar, subdued lighting and seating booths framed by colourful stained glass may say 'pub' but the menu begs to differ, offering a long and exciting list of simple, traditional dishes from around the world – a creamy Cypriot hummus, for example, or slow cooked Mediterranean lamb casserole. More conservative tastes are catered for with the likes of surf and turf and rump steak au poivre in the evenings or daytime dishes such as Irish steak and ale pie or Welsh Lamb stew. A colourful array of international arts and crafts (all for sale) extends into the new shop at the back of the restaurant – also a holistic therapy centre – where you'll find crystals, herbs, candles and clothing. Don't miss the chance to explore this, or the tranquil garden with its flowers, driftwood furniture and trickling fountain. There is an apt leaning towards local, organic ingredients and wholefoods, with excellent choices for vegetarians, though an enjoyable side salad of mixed leaves, sprouted beans and seeds might benefit from a spot of dressing. Finish with home-made desserts (perhaps a comforting bread, butter and marmalade pudding) or sundaes made with luxury Belgian ice cream.

Owners: Lesley Lewis & John Glasby Chef: Lesley Lewis
Open: L Mon – Sat 10.30 – 5.00 D Fri – Sat 6.30 – 9.15
Closed: Christmas Day/Bank Holidays Seats: 100 L £15 D £25

Visa/Mastercard/Diners/Switch/Delta  Map reference 60

# Hawarden

## Brasserie

**Hawarden CH5 3DH**
**Tel: 01244 536353**
**Email: thebrasserie@hotmail.com**
**www.brasserie1016.com/hawarden**
On main road, through Hawarden, between the school and castle

Not the most enticing of buildings from the outside – plain whitewashed façade with half-frosted windows and a busy roadside location – but step inside and it's evident why the residents of Hawarden love this super little brasserie. The place has a modern, fresh feel, with its light walls, wooden floors, subtle spotlighting and chunky wooden furnishings, the atmosphere is warm and friendly and the service is attentive and courteous. The winning formula that draws the crowds combines an express lunch menu and a bargain prix-fixe menu with a lively, eclectic and up-to-the-minute carte that delivers good Mediterranean influenced dishes. Starters include baked crab, leek and Parmesan tart with caper and lemon crème fraiche and glazed salmon, potato and Gruyere cheese terrine with a mango, coriander and red onion salsa. Follow, perhaps, with fresh sea bass fillets on creamy, well cooked lemon thyme and mascarpone risotto, crowned with asparagus in tempura batter and served with a faultless hollandaise. Round off with a classic pudding – strawberry shortbread cheesecake – a selection of Cheshire Farm ice creams, or a plate of farmhouse cheeses. Thirty or so well-chosen wines.

Owners: Neal Bates & Mark Jones Chef: Mark Jones Open: L Sun – Fri 12.00 – 2.00 D all week 6.00 – 9.30 Closed: Boxing Day/New Years Day Seats: 25 L £12 D £19.50

Visa/Mastercard/Amex/Switch/Delta   Map reference **61**

**26 Lion Street, Hay-on-Wye HR3 5AD**
**Tel: 01497 820841**
**Email: info@oldblacklion.co.uk**
**www.oldblacklion.co.uk**
Turn right from the main car park and take 2nd turning on left

## Old Black Lion

### Hay-on-Wye

Oliver Cromwell stayed here and this predominantly 17th century coaching inn has bags of old world charm but also some first rate cooking served in the oak-beamed dining room and in the King Richard bar. Chef Peter Bridges delivers an impressive European menu to the throng of discerning diners that regularly descend on this upmarket inn. Food is freshly prepared to order and there may be delays but the well presented dishes are well worth waiting for. Locally reared meats are used well and seasonal vegetables and herbs come straight from the pub garden. The chalkboard menu in the bar offers reliable favourites like a rich and memorable steak and kidney pie, Moroccan lamb or a classic fish pie. From the more elaborate dining room menu (also available in the bar in the evenings), follow home-made breads and tomato and lovage soup, with saddle of Welsh Lamb with herb crust and lamb jus, pan-fried fallow venison on a parsnip purée tart with blackberry and gin sauce, or halibut fillet with spring onion and bacon mash. Round off with a delicious summer pudding. Super, efficient service and decent house wines by the bottle and glass.

**H**

Owner: Vanessa King Chef: Peter Bridges Open: all week
L 12.00 – 2.30 D 6.30 – 9.30 Closed: Christmas Day/Boxing Day,
2nd & 3rd weeks of Jan Seats: 60 L £20 D £25

20  10  P  V  r

C  Visa/Mastercard/Switch/Delta  Map reference

## Pear Tree

**6 Church Street, Hay-on-Wye, Powys HR3 5DQ**
Tel: 01497 820777
Email: info@peartreeathay.co.uk
www.peartreeathay.co.uk
Opposite Hay Cinema Book Shop

An attractive townhouse on the edge of the town centre, the Pear Tree has established an excellent reputation in recent years and is now a key destination for visitors to Hay in search of good food. There is a homely atmosphere to the place, partly because the network of rooms that make up the premises still resemble a rather stylish house. Drinks can be taken in the lounge on comfortable sofas, whilst the food is served in the scarlet red dining room, the shelves of which are lined with an impressive array of cookbooks. The menu is relatively short (often a good sign) and is well-judged in terms of balancing flavours and styles. Amongst the starters a superior version of a classic chicken Caesar salad is lifted by a slight spiciness to the dressing and Thai fishcakes are another example of the familiar being done very well. Main courses are generous in flavour as well as quantity and might include a sticky braised shank of Welsh Lamb with mash, tamarind and dates. There is a relaxed and friendly style to service and the whole experience is complemented by a wine list that offers plenty of choice without breaking the bank.

Owners: Rod & Penny Lewis Chef: Rod Lewis Open: Tues – Sat D only 7.00 – 9.00 Closed: Christmas Day/Boxing Day & 2nd week of June Seats: 34 D £22.50

Visa/Mastercard/Switch/Delta Map reference 63

**Knighton LD7 1LT**
Tel: 01547 528632
Email: hotel@milebrook.kc3ltd.co.uk
www.milebrookhouse.co.uk
2 miles east of Knighton on the Ludlow road

The comfortable creeper-clad house, built in the 17th century, is more solid than grand, built for living in rather than showing off, with a pleasing domestic scale and personable service. Evenings run to a simple format, starting with something to nibble over an aperitif in the bar, followed by a three course set-price dinner in the charming double dining room. Here french doors give access to the glorious four-acre garden, its sheltered terrace and kitchen garden whose produce supplies vegetables, soft fruits, salads and herbs in summer. Beryl's dependable hand on the tiller is appreciated, especially her influence in the kitchen. The cooking is carefully balanced between the country house idiom of terrine of pork, chicken livers and pistachio with Cumberland sauce or breast of free-range chicken stuffed with Shropshire blue cheese and pine nuts with port wine sauce and gutsier modern combinations such as salad of poached egg and frazzled home-made chorizo, and pan-fried sea mullet served with roasted peppers, salsa verde and tapenade. Fruit and cream are popular combinations for pudding, fresh fruit salad pavlova, for example, with raspberry coulis. The list of international wines is fairly priced.

Owners: Rodney & Beryl Marsden Chef: Lee Jones Open: L Tues – Sun 12.00 – 1.30 D Tues – Sat 7.00 – 9.00 Seats: 35 L £12.50 D £26.50

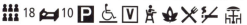

C Visa/Mastercard/Diners/Switch/Delta  Map reference

# Cors

**Newbridge Road, Laugharne,
Carmarthenshire SA33 4SH
Tel. 01994 427219**

In Laugharne, turn left at the Mariners pub (from Pendine), turn right (from St Clears)

As soon as you make the approach through an exotic bog garden it's clear that The Cors is special. Nick Priestland (artist, gardener, chef) has created a world apart – a bohemian, romantic restaurant in the Victorian house that is also his home. Wander the grounds before your meal or settle in the bar and enjoy the carefully chosen music. Quirky furniture, abstract art and plenty of candlelight set a stylish scene but the tiny dining room, with its deep red walls and huge mirrors, is the star of the show. The cooking is unpretentious but inspired, with a strong emphasis on quality, seasonal and local produce. A memorable starter of a potato and dill pancake with local salmon and mascarpone offers a full spectrum of taste and texture, as does the local goats' cheese, grilled to perfection and served with bruschetta, roasted peppers, sun-blushed tomatoes and dressed salad leaves. Main courses could include pan fried calf's liver, sage and caramelised red onion gravy or tournedos of beef fillet, cooked precisely as requested, with a red wine jus and a kick of green peppercorn. Service is charming and relaxed in all senses. The shortish but quality packed wine list supports the menu well.

Owner: Nick Priestland Chef: Nick Priestland Open: Thurs – Sat D only 7.00 – 9.30 Closed: Christmas Day & 1st 2 weeks in Nov Seats: 24 D £24 20 2 r

Map reference 65

**East Marsh, Laugharne,
Carmarthenshire SA33 4RS
Tel: 01994 427417
www.hurst-house.co.uk**
Go through Laugharne & Broadway
and follow signs for Hurst House

## Laugharne

Metropolitan chic in an idyllic rural setting is the order of the day at Matt Roberts and Neil Morrissey's much reported Hurst House. The reference points include sophisticated bold colour schemes, stylish contemporary design and an approach to cuisine which is rather more Notting Hill than rural West Wales. Whilst dishes are presented in a distinctly contemporary, urban style, the shopping is done locally and fine local foods such as salt marsh lamb (braised and served with olive oil mash) feature prominently. Fish is often deftly handled and can appear in comforting classics like a delicious fishcake with watercress sauce. The bar is very much the heart of this hotel and guests who appreciate the modish surroundings congregate to sample the fine selection of drinks and cocktails on offer. Smartly attired staff are eager to please although a little more attention to the fine points of service might be more in keeping with these slick surroundings. Make time to explore the extensive grounds which - while still a work in progress – are becoming an important focal point for the hotel. The rooms are exeptionally stylish so there is no need to rush home after a late night cocktail.

**L**

Owners: Hurst House Farm Ltd Chef: Dion Tidmarsh Open: all week
L 12.00 – 3.00 D 7.00 – 10.00 Seats: 60  L £25.85 D £30.85

C  Visa/Mastercard/Amex/Switch/Delta  Map reference

# Stable Door

**Market Lane, Laugharne
Carmarthenshire SA33 4SB
Tel: 01994 427777**
Behind clock tower, second restaurant on right, down cobbled lane

This stone built restaurant and wine bar sits in historic premises just behind Laugharne's main thoroughfare. The atmosphere is casual and relaxed and this is probably not the right place to take aging relatives intent on a formal family meal with white tablecloth trappings. Sit in the verdant conservatory overlooking the garden and it's vista over the ruins of Laugharne castle and enjoy a carefully prepared meal with few cheffy pretensions but bags of honest flavour. Owner Wendy Joy is a real character and you are as likely to find her beavering away in the kitchen as attending to her guests needs front of house. Modern classics like crab cakes are given an oriental reworking with the addition of coconut and sweet chilli sauce and there are vegetarian friendly dishes on every menu. Try the cumin and coriander scented falafels with hummus and pitta bread to start perhaps followed by a spicy Thai green curry with vegetables and coconut cream. The Stable Door has a loyal following for Sunday lunch with traditional roasts given a fresh twist by careful selection of local lamb and beef. The wine list is great value and does offer some novel choices seldom found elsewhere.

Owner: Wendy Joy Chef: Wendy Joy Open: Sun L 12.30 – 3.00 Thurs – Sat D 7.00 – 9.30 Closed: 4 weeks in Jan Seats: 65
L £13.95 D £20.22
30
Visa/Mastercard/Switch/Delta Map reference 67

**Llanarmon Dyffryn Ceiriog,**
**Near Llangollen, Denbighshire LL20 7LD**
**Tel: 01691 600665**
Email: gowestarms@aol.com
www.thewestarms.co.uk
Go west on the B4500 from Chirk, hotel at end of the valley

In the dim and distant past this was a simple drovers inn, but a country hotel has emerged over the years, taking full advantage of a spellbinding location to draw folk from near and far. There may be nothing to shock the unwary on the blackboard for lunch in the informal bar, or indeed on the fixed-price, daily changing dinner menu served in the traditional dining room, but there's a good balance of fish, meat, game and vegetable options, and the silver dome service (even in the bar) complements the beams and polished oak furniture. The repertoire might run from lunchtime leek and potato soup to grilled Ceiriog trout with almonds and vegetables, or a platter of salami with watercress salad and tomato and tarragon vinaigrette, to fillet of Welsh organic lamb for dinner. On the whole, evening main courses favour traditional treatments such as Champagne butter sauce with steamed fillet of wild turbot, or red wine, wild mushrooms and truffle oil with breast of guinea fowl, whilst desserts mobilise a lot of cream, whether Eton mess with fresh local strawberries, or iced cheesecake parfait. A blackboard in the bar lists 10 wines by the glass.

Owners: Gill & Geoff Leigh-Ford  Chef: Grant Williams  Open: L Sun 12.00 – 2.00  D all week  7.00 – 9.00  Seats: 30  L £18  D £32

8  15  P  V  

C  Visa/Mastercard/Switch/Delta  Map reference

# Y Bistro

**Llanberis**

**43 – 45 High Street, Llanberis, Gwynedd LL55 4EU**
**Tel: 01286 871278**
**Email: ybistro@fsbdial.co.uk**
**www.ybistro.co.uk**
In the centre of the village by the tourist office

Husband and wife team Danny and Nerys Roberts are celebrating 25 years at their friendly, informal restaurant, formerly a Victorian corner shop, in the town centre. Although little has changed inside the comfortable bistro over the years, Nerys's bilingual menus have moved with the times and Y Bistro is regarded as a pioneer of real food in this part of Wales.

The cooking is distinctly Welsh with French overtones, with full use made of local mountain lamb, locally reared pork, Welsh Black beef and seasonal game. Follow freshly baked bread with a rich Mediterranean fish soup infused with tomato and garlic, or chicken liver and brandy parfait with spicy apple chutney. Main courses usually include local lamb, perhaps a perfectly pink-roasted best end with polenta mash and blackberry gravy, and a plump, juicy breast of chicken stuffed with Welsh cheese and wrapped in Carmarthen ham and roasted with onions. Flavours shine through and accompanying vegetables are imaginative and well cooked. Round off with local blackberry and apple crumble, rich dark organic chocolate pudding with white chocolate sauce, or a platter of Welsh cheeses.

Owners: Danny & Nerys Roberts   Chef: Nerys Roberts
Open: Tues – Sat D only 7.30 – 9.45   Closed: 1st two weeks Jan
Seats: 40   D £28

Visa/Mastercard/Switch/Delta   Map reference 69

**Llanddarog, Carmarthenshire SA32 8NS**
**Tel: 01267 275330**
9 miles West of M4 junction 49
on B4310

With a broad and varied customer base, the Butchers Arms is as popular for its home-made chips as its restaurant fare. Hundreds of years old (nobody knows quite how old), it's the best kind of country pub – clean, friendly and rambling. Its reputation for good food predates gastro pubs and perhaps because of this it remains untouched by rag rolling, paint stripper or abstract art. Instead, the walls bear musical instruments and maritime memorabilia. David and Mavis James took on the Butchers 23 years ago and have pretty much stuck to the same successful formula throughout. The menu offers a down to earth jaunt through local produce such as cockles (with bacon and laverbread), lamb (slow roasted) and fresh fish. David's cooking is hearty and generous: a starter of deep fried brie provides more brie than you'd usually put on a cheeseboard, oozing from a light, crisp batter. It will always be more rustic than refined but (as with a deeply savoury soup packed with translucent, thickly sliced onions) this can be a joy. For dessert, revert to childhood with thumb sucking comfort food such as sticky jammy roll and custard. Wines include a few by the glass and about eight by the bottle.

Owners: David & Mavis James Chef: David James Open: Mon – Sat L 12.00 – 2.20 D 6.00 (5.00 on Sat) – 9.30 Closed: Christmas Day/Boxing Day Seats: 65 L £13 D £22

23

C Visa/Mastercard/Switch/Delta  Map reference

## Palé Hall

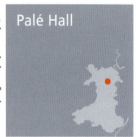

**Palé Estate, Llandderfel, Bala, Gwynedd LL23 7PS**
**Tel: 01678 530285**
Email: enquiries@palehall.co.uk
www.palehall.co.uk
Situated just off the B4401, Corwen to Bala road, 4 miles from Llandrillo, signposted from main road

This baronial mansion is in a wonderful spot, overlooking parkland in a quiet and picturesque setting close to Bala Lake. It has a fine wood-panelled entrance hall and lots of heavy Victorian ornamentation feature in the various sitting rooms and gracious dining room. A lot of work undoubtedly goes into producing elaborate dishes, for example sautéed chicken livers are layered with potato, bound in chive oil, wrapped in Parma ham and served with brioche. This constitutes the first of three courses at dinner and might be followed by fillet of brill with a coarse fennel and leek pâté, roast baby vine tomatoes and pesto cappuccino sauce, then warm croissant orange and chocolate pudding with lemon Anglaise. Such an isolated spot does mean that on a weekday you could be the only visitors for lunch, which is served in the cosy confines of the Bala Kitchen, but don't let that put you off. The three course, no-choice deal is a steal at £13 and could run to broccoli and Stilton soup, rump steak with lentils, sweet potato and fresh vegetables and a superb walnut and treacle tart. Wines are nicely varied in style and reasonably priced.

Owner: Saul Nahed  Chef: Karl Cheetam  Open: all week
L 12.00 – 1.30  D 7.00 – 8.30  Seats: 43  L £15  D £30

20  17  P  V

C  Visa/Mastercard/Switch/Delta  Map reference **71**

**Llandegla, Wrexham LL11 3AL**
**Tel: 01978 790434**
Email: info@bodidrishall.com
www.bodidrishall.com
Off A5104 Chester – Corwen Road

More than five hundred years of history is embodied within the walls of this creeper-clad country house hotel. Approached along a mile-long drive and set in mature parkland with a trout lake, Bodidris boasts huge fireplaces, fine oak panelling and a baronial dining room that looks out towards Llandegla Moor. Chef Kevin Steele utilizes fresh local and organic ingredients in preparing the well balanced, five course set dinner menu and the exceptional value two course lunch menu, which complement the warm hospitality and relaxed atmosphere of this comfortable hotel. Follow canapés in the lounge with a starter of home cured gravadlax with blinis and pink peppercorn dressing, or a generous slice of rich duck, ham and wild mushroom roulade, served on a large white plate, with a redcurrant and ginger sauce. For main course there may be pepper roast monkfish with wilted greens, langoustine risotto and red pepper oil and herb-crusted rack of lamb served with a light garlic cream and berry tartlet. Organic vegetables from the kitchen garden may include courgettes, cauliflower and green beans. Puddings include a delicious light and creamy, lavender infused crème brûlée, or opt for the cheese platter which includes several Welsh cheese.

Owners: David & Stephanie Booth Chef: Kevin Steele Open: all week
L 12.00 – 2.00 D 7.00 – 9.30 Seats: 65 🍽 L £15.90 D £29.85

👥 65 🛏 9 🅿 ♿ Ⓥ 👶r 🌿 ✗ 🍴 ♨

C Visa/Mastercard/Amex/Switch Map reference

# Angel Inn & Capel Bach Bistro

Llandeilo

62 Rhosmaen Street, Llandeilo, Carmarthenshire SA19 6EN
Tel: 01558 822765
Email: capelbach@hotmail.com
www.angelbistro.co.uk
Take the A40 into Llandeilo, in the centre of town

A womb-like underground room at the back of the smart Angel pub, Y Capel Bach dates back to the 1700s. Its stylish décor includes tapestry covered banqueting chairs, uneven terracotta-red walls and dozens of charming old photographs of carefully posed families. The regular menu is modern British in style, so expect classic British ingredients with a subtle international twist – tender topside of Welsh Lamb, for instance, stuffed with mozzarella on spinach with a rosemary and red wine jus, or pink Barbary duck breast on a stir-fried vegetable base in hoi sin sauce. The core menu is supplemented on certain days by theme menus; Monday and Tuesday are steak and grill nights and Thursday is Thai night. Dishes are attractively presented and generously portioned. Though there is the occasional inconsistency (such as green beans cooked rather too 'al dente') the overall experience is enjoyable and the staff are friendly and eager to please. Desserts are a strength, so leave room for the likes of summer pudding or a very memorable and decadent Mars bar cheesecake.

Owners: Paul & Tracey Kindred  Chefs: Paul Kindred & Paul Owen
Open: Mon – Sat L 11.30 – 2.30 D 6.30 – 9.30  Closed: Christmas Day
Seats: 44  L £10 D £23
68

Visa/Mastercard/Amex/Diners/Switch/Delta  Map reference 73

**Llandenny, Near Usk**
**Monmouthshire NP15 1DL**
**Tel: 01291 690800**
Llandenny is situated centrally, between Raglan and Usk

Village pubs have to work ever harder to stay viable and the Raglan Arms has had its own ups and downs over the years. Enthusiastic owners with a determination to create something worth a journey can work wonders though and that's been the story at the Raglan Arms. Ian and Carol Black have turned this into a pub that both serves the locality and attracts those from much further afield drawn by the combination of good food, generous hospitality and the charm of the building itself. Daily changing blackboard menus carry the bulk of the dishes which offer plenty in the way of variety but share in common, freshness, big flavours and ample quantities. Classics like seafood risotto are handled with real understanding but more rustic efforts like lambs' liver, bacon and onions are treated with similar care and it's good to see that proper attention is given to items like bread. The Raglan Pie has the makings of a legend and reminds you how good a properly made hand-raised pie can be. There are some good real ales to be had together with a brief but pocket-friendly list of wines.

Owners: Ian & Carol Black  Chef: Ian Black  Open: Tues – Sun
L 12.00 – 2.00 Tues – Sat  D 7.00 – 9.30  Seats: 52  L £15  D £20
24
Visa/Mastercard/Switch/Delta  Map reference

# Leadon's Brasserie

**Llandevaud**

**Foresters Oaks Hotel, Chepstow Road, Llandevaud, Newport NP18 2AA**
**Tel: 01633 400260**
Coldra roundabout junction off M4, onto A48, through Langstone, pub on right

Enjoy an aperitif in the comfortable lounge with its squashy sofas before venturing through to the smart African themed brasserie proper for a meal as far reaching in its reference points as the room itself. A typical starter could be the fusion classic seared scallops with chilli jam and crème fraîche or perhaps kiln roasted salmon with smoked paprika aïoli and a red chilli gazpacho dressing – make no mistake the flavours are bold here. Main courses may take in the bestselling rump or sirloin steaks with classic béarnaise sauce or a well-crafted assiette of chicken where several cooking methods jostle for attention on the same plate. Diners have a wealth of choice and this can, on occasion, be a little too much for the kitchen to keep up with. Lunch is a real bargain and can be taken in the stylish bar as well as the more formal brasserie itself. Puddings are similarly complex; pannacotta comes Grand Marnier scented with candied peel and orange crème Anglaise, or for those without a sweet tooth try the selection of well kept cheeses served with panetonne, grapes and Bath Oliver biscuits.
A thoughtfully selected wine list offers some real bargains and staff are keen to advise with selection.

Owner: Wayne Leadon Chefs: Andrew Reagan & Wayne Leadon
Open: L Tues – Sun 12.00 – 2.00  D Tues – Sat 6.00 – 10.00  Closed: Christmas Day/ Boxing Day, Jan 1st – 14th  Seats: 80  L £12.95 D £24  30  6

Visa/Mastercard/Amex/Switch/Delta    Map reference 75

**Llandrillo LL21 0ST**
**Tel: 01490 440264**
**Email: tyddynllan@compuserve.com**
**www.tyddynllan.co.uk**
From A5 in Corwen, take B4401 to Llandrillo, on right hand side towards Bala

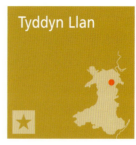

Comfort has been given a high priority at this grey stone Georgian country house where good taste and a sense of restraint combine with a luxuriously spacious feel. Evenings begin on sofas in an oriental rug-strewn lounge, where you nibble olives, roasted nuts and canapés while studying the fixed-price dinner menu, then continue in the well-dressed dining room with lots of lazy space between tables. Bryan Webb's cooking is a meeting point for traditional and contemporary ideas and the relative simplicity and directness of his food exposes the quality of the buying and his considerable skills. It is this, rather than brash spicing and whiz-bang flavour combinations, that creates the excitement. When grilled lobster is combined with ginger, coriander and lime butter, that is very much an exception to the rule. More typical is griddled scallops with vegetable relish and rocket, or rack of local lamb with herb crust, summer vegetables and dauphinoise potatoes. Summer pudding is an explosion of rich, tart fruit offset by an intense blackcurrant sorbet. Service is slightly formal but knowledgeable, and wines combine interest and quality at a fair range of prices, with 17 by the glass.

True Taste hospitality Silver 2003-4

Owners: Bryan & Susan Webb  Chef: Bryan Webb  Open: Fri – Sun (Tues – Thurs by arrangement) L 12.30 – 2.00 D all week, (booking essential) 7.00 – 9.30  Closed: 2 weeks in Jan  Seats: 35
L £24 D £35  40  13

Visa/Mastercard/Switch/Delta  Map reference 76

## Bodysgallen Hall

**Llandudno, Conwy LL30 1RS**
**Tel: 01492 584466**
**Email: info@bodysgallen.com**
**www.bodysgallen.com**
2 miles from Llandudno

The 17th century house luxuriates in 200 acres of gardens and parkland on a hill above Llandudno. Aperitifs in the oak-panelled hall or first-floor drawing room and (for gentlemen) jacket and tie at dinner in the dining room, add up to a textbook country house hotel. In this case, however, one is unlikely to be overwhelmed, thanks in part to the pleasant staff. The chef John Williams (who achieved a Michelin star at his Shrewsbury restaurant Sol) took over the kitchen in November 2003 and now regales North Wales with a beguiling repertoire and an assured skill that puts classic French techniques at the service of modern ideas. There is some luxury, a lot of craftsmanship and produce of the highest order, but above all flavour is used positively, providing a spicy melon chutney to accompany a twice-baked cheese soufflé, or ginger cream sauce and crab fritter with a fillet of local sea bass. Lunch is a shade simpler than dinner, but is still likely to include terrine of new season lamb with toasted brioche and baby leek, fillet of Welsh Black beef, light carrot gateau and red wine and thyme sauce, with champagne and Bodysgallen berry jelly to finish. Wines have been selected with an eye for quality with several by the glass.

Owners: Historic House Hotels Chef: John Williams Open: all Week L 12.30 – 1.45 D 7.00 – 9.30 Closed: 24th – 27th Dec, 30th Dec – 2nd Jan Seats: 55 L £22 D £38

40  35  P  &  V  r

C  Visa/Mastercard/Switch/Delta  Map reference  77

**7 Church Walks, Llandudno LL30 2HD**
**Tel: 01492 875315**
**Email: gillian@jephcott71.fsnet.co.uk**
Main street, Mostyn head to far end, Great Orme, turn right into Church Walks

Just two minutes walk from the seafront and tucked away among the dozens of hotels and B&Bs, this basement restaurant is identified by the canopy over the stairs. Inside, this small restaurant has a comfortable cottage like appearance; wooden banquettes with squashy cushions, slate tiled floor, wooden beams and the kitchen open to the dining room. The menu is quite extensive with ten choices of starter and main course including several suitable for vegetarians. Grilled garlic field mushrooms are topped with sun-dried tomatoes, roasted red peppers, herb couscous and ricotta. The odd eastern flavour appears here and there as in the Vietnamese style hot and sour fishcakes with chillies, lemongrass, coriander and nam pla. More traditionally, smoked haddock chowder is a hearty mix of leeks, potatoes, white wine and cream, and Welsh Lamb comes stuffed with apricots and rosemary with a red wine jus, or slow cooked with black pudding and chicken in a rich Cognac, garlic and wine gravy. That old bistro classic calf's liver is served nicely pink on rösti potato with a redcurrant jus. Puddings stick with the traditional, fruit crumble, creme brûlée and toffee pudding in a caramel sauce will not disappoint.

Owners: Donald & Gillian Hadwin  Chef: Donald Hadwin
Open: Tues – Sat D only 5.30 - 10.30  Closed: Christmas Day/Bank Holidays  Seats: 50  D £24.95

**30**  **P**  **V**

**C**  Visa/Mastercard/Amex/Switch/Delta  Map reference  **78**

# St Tudno

**Promenade, Llandudno LL30 2LP**
**Tel: 01492 874411**
**Email: sttudnohotel@btinternet.com**
**www.st-tudno.co.uk**

Follow the promenade until the war memorial (T junction), turn right, 150 yards on left hand side

Set in a terrace of imposing Victorian houses facing the promenade, Martin and Janette Bland's rightly celebrated seaside hotel feels more like a country house within. At lunch the kitchen allows itself to concentrate on main course cooking-to-order by serving predominantly cold starters along the lines of salad of grilled goats' cheese with crispy bacon, tomatoes and olives, or locally smoked salmon with lemon. The centre of gravity is somewhere in France, hence excellent roast rump of lamb with garlic mash potato, spinach and rosemary jus and fricassée of chicken with galette potato and red cabbage confit. Dinner is more ambitious, but the choice continues to run along classical lines with a few twists from chef Stephen Duffy, such as a pastry case of kidneys and bubble and squeak to accompany roast rump of Welsh Lamb and teaming braised fillet of halibut with vanilla and pernod velouté, rosemary potato purée and buttered spinach. Pear and almond charlotte with raspberries and a chocolate sauce is one of five desserts that might also include iced blackberry yoghurt with a warm apple soup. Wine is a strength and the impressive list is well worth taking time over.

Owners: Martin & Janette Bland Chef: Stephen Duffy Open: all week L 12.30 – 1.45 D 7.00 – 9.15 Seats: 60 L £16.50 D £38.50
18 P V r (Lunch only)
C Visa/Mastercard/Amex/Diners/Switch/Delta Map reference 79

**5 Penbryn Cottages, High Street, Llanfyllin, Powys SY22 5AP**
**Tel: 01691 648604**
In main High street of Llanfyllin

This unassuming, brick sixteenth-century cottage is a local favourite, although it also draws a following from further afield. It's a relaxed place with a friendly but professional atmosphere, run for fifteen years by Mark and Felicity Seager. They are clearly happy, with Felicity running front of house and Mark working single-handed in the kitchen, his cooking somewhat more refined than the bistro ambience of bare wood tables, beams and exposed brick walls may suggest. The focus is on sound culinary principles, traditional cooking methods and impeccable sourcing. Fillet steak is served with brandy and green peppercorn sauce, for example, sautéed chicken breast with port and cream sauce and a trio of fish comes with white wine, cream and cheese sauce. Red meats such as lamb are cooked pink and the timing certainly suited a tasty roast rack of Welsh Lamb that came with a Dijon and herb crust and good, fresh vegetables. The short, set-price menu can open with a satisfying sun-dried tomato risotto, or some simple grilled sardines and finish with apple and blackberry crumble, or lemon posset and blackcurrant sauce. Wines are a passion, well selected and reasonably priced, with plenty of half bottles and a decent choice by the glass.

Owners: Felicity & Mark Seager  Chef: Mark Seager  Open: Thurs – Sun L 11.00 – 2.15 Wed – Sat D 7.00 – 9.00  Closed: Christmas Day & 2 weeks Oct/Nov  Seats: 22  L £14.65 D £23

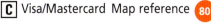
C  Visa/Mastercard  Map reference

# Lake Country House

**Llangammarch Wells, Powys LD4 4BS**
**Tel: 01591 620202**
**Email: info@lakecountryhouse.co.uk**
www.lakecountryhouse.co.uk
From Builth Wells, take A483 Llandovery, in Garth turn left & follow signs

The setting in 50 acres of grounds is undiluted country house, with deep sofas, swagged curtains and highly polished furniture leaving guests in no doubt as to its Victorian credentials. Old-fashioned service contributes to the 'Upstairs Downstairs' feel and the dining room is terribly proper, with immaculate table linen and sparkling glasses. In keeping with the surroundings, a mainstream style of country house cooking is offered in the form of fixed-price four course menus at lunch and dinner. It is not, however, entirely averse to incorporating the odd contemporary flourish. There may be an escabeche of salmon and monkfish with coriander, for example, and fillet of halibut with herb and langoustine risotto, braised fennel, cherry tomatoes and grapefruit butter sauce, but the centre of gravity remains very much in the vein of country game terrine with saffron pear chutney, or fillet of Welsh Beef with dauphinoise potatoes, red onion compote, wild mushrooms and truffle jus. To finish there may be Malibu pannacotta with pineapple sorbet. Wines are strong in the major French regions.

Owner: Jean-Pierre Mifsud  Chef: Sean Cullingford  Open: all week
L 12.15 – 2.00  D 7.15 – 9.15  Seats: 50  L £23.50  D £37.50
50  19
Visa/Mastercard/Amex/Diners/Switch/Delta  Map reference 81

**Dee Lane, Llangollen LL20 8PN**
**Tel: 01978 869555**
corn.mill@brunningandprice.co.uk
www.cornmill-llangollen.co.uk
Right on the river Dee

# Cornmill

## Llangollen

Little can prepare you for the stunning location and the quite superb renovation of this late 18th century mill smack beside the rushing waters of the River Dee. Expect three floors, all gloriously restored and oozing original charm and character, with wooden floors, old machinery, huge exposed beams, thick stone walls and a working water wheel turning behind the bar and viewed from upstairs through glass panels in the floor. Add an eclectic mix of old furnishings, a dining area with picture windows with river and mountain views and wonderful alfresco terrace suspended over the Dee and filled with upmarket teak furniture and you have a stylish, modern pub geared to both local drinkers and discerning diners. Food is taken very seriously here, the all-day menu listing classic favourites (Welsh pork and herb sausages with spring onion mash and herb gravy) alongside imaginative pub meals, perhaps a generous dish of tender shoulder of lamb with spring vegetables, roast potatoes and herb gravy. Puddings include a light and creamy bara brith and butter pudding with apricot sauce. Salads, Welsh cheese ploughman's and sandwiches are served throughout the day. Cracking real ales from micro-breweries, interesting wines of the month and a blissful, music-free atmosphere complete the picture.

Owners: Brunning & Price Chef: Andy Greenhouse Open: L & D all week 12.00 – 9.30 Closed: Christmas Day/Boxing Day for lunch, New Years Day Eve for dinner Seats: 177  L £23 D £23

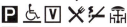
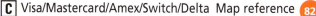 Visa/Mastercard/Amex/Switch/Delta  Map reference

## Peterstone Court

**Llanhamlach, Brecon LD3 7YB**
**Tel: 01874 665387**
**Email: info@peterstone-court.com**
**www.peterstone-court.com**
On the A40, between Abergavenny and Brecon

Peterstone Court is the newest outpost in the growing hospitality empire that also takes in Nantyffin Cider Mill (see entry). Externally very much the country house but the stylish contemporary interior owes nothing to the chintz loving school of thought which often informs the interior decoration of similar properties. Chef Daniel James has a solid pedigree and he brings a thoughtful, unfussy style of cuisine to the table. Start with perhaps a classic French fish soup with smoked paprika rouille, Gruyere cheese and crisp croutons. Meats come from the family farm at Llangynidr and are always in prime condition. Try, perhaps, a roast loin of lamb with pea purée and a lightly minted red wine jus. Vegetables are carefully handled and a range of well chosen side dishes supplements the menu. Royale potatoes with cheese or Jersey new potatoes in season make admirable main dish companions. Pastry is a further strength: who can resist a well made rice pudding, especially when accompanied by gently poached summer berry compote? A well chosen wine list completes the picture with good value house wines at a bargain price.

Owners: G & J Bridgeman, S Gerrard  Chef: Daniel James
Open: all week L 12.00 – 2.30 D 7.00 – 9.30  Seats: 40  L £19 D £19
135  12
Visa/Mastercard/Amex/Diners/Switch/Delta  Map reference 83

**Llanrhidian, Gower, Swansea SA3 1EH**
**Tel: 01792 390015**
**Email: ian@thebennetts12.freeserve.co.uk**
**www.thewelcometotown.co.uk**
Follow sign from main road in Llanrhidian

# Welcome to Town Inn

## Llanrhidian

Situated on the margins of the Gower's bountiful salt marsh coastline Ian Bennett's fine restaurant is ideally placed to make the most of the cornucopia of fine ingredients available on his doorstep. The room itself strikes a slightly incongruous note as the setting for such high quality eating as it is a little reminiscent of a country tearoom but diners entering the cottage like interior are rewarded with a dining experience that would grace any surroundings. Front of house is supervised by Ian's wife Jay who greets expectant diners as if they are old friends. With the coastline so close, as one would expect, seafood is a particular strength but carnivores will be delighted with the quality of local salt marsh lamb. This is a chef who has the good sense to let his fine supplies speak for themselves – witness a delightful starter of simply seared locally dived scallops served with a dressed mixed leaf salad and a drizzle of aged balsamic. What could be more enjoyable than kicking back on a summers evening with a main course of half a grilled lobster with tarragon and shallot butter, crispy chips and a dressed green salad, throw in a glass of crisp Muscadet from the thoughtfully constructed wine list – a recipe for dining bliss.

Owners: Jay & Ian Bennett Chef: Ian Bennett Open: Tues – Sun L 12.00 – 2.00 D Tues – Sat 7.00 – 9.30 Closed: Tues in Winter months Christmas Day/Boxing Day, 1 week in Oct, last 2 weeks Feb Seats: 40

L £15 D £30

C Visa/Mastercard/Switch Map reference

# Seiont Manor

**Llanrug, Caernarfon LL55 2AQ**
**Tel: 01286 673366**
**Email: seiontmanor@handpicked.co.uk**
**www.handpicked.co.uk/seiontmanor**

2 miles outside of Caernarfon, on the Llanberis Road, just outside the village of Llanrug

Posh surroundings these may be but the overwhelming feeling at Seiont Manor is that of warm welcome rather than grand hotel stuffiness. The stylishly elegant restaurant is clutter free and boasts a magnificent view over the rolling countryside. Take aperitifs in one of the clubby lounges and bars before sitting down to some assured cooking. The cooking of Martin Williams is in many ways like the room itself, not over complicated and presented with elegant simplicity. Start with smoked trout, pickled samphire and lemon dressing or perhaps a wood pigeon and red onion tart served with an earthy cider and apple chutney. Loin of venison may come with cabbage confit, local bresaola and roast onion. Those with a sweet tooth are not neglected and reworked classics are the order of the day where puddings are concerned. An eggy bread and butter pudding may come with sticky butterscotch sauce or try, perhaps, simple poached pear with chocolate sauce and banoffi ice cream. The wine list has a full range of classic bottles and prices can reach stratospheric heights but house wine is keenly priced.

Owners: Hand Picked Hotels  Chef: Martin Williams  Open: all week
L 12.00 – 2.00 D 7.00 – 9.30 Seats: 60  L £13.50 D £26.75
30  28

Visa/Mastercard/Amex/Diners/Switch/Delta  Map reference 85

32 – 34 Heol yr Orsaf, Llanrwst,
Conwy LL26 0BT
Tel: 01492 641188/640215
Email: info@blasarfwyd.com
www.blasarfwyd.com
On the A470, 200 metres to the North
of Llanrwst Square

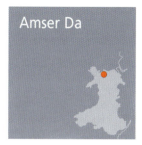

With his hugely successful Blas ar Fwyd Delicatessen and Blas ar Win Wine Merchants and his popular Amser Da Restaurant facing each other on Heol Yr Orsaf, Deiniol ap Dafydd is a big figure in tiny Llanrwst. Well respected as a supplier of quality Welsh and continental foods since he opened his delicatessen in 1988, the all-day café-come-evening bistro was the natural progression for ambitious Deiniol. Amser Da has a smart brasserie feel, with coffee bar in the front, bistro-restaurant with bold French murals beyond, and a function space upstairs. The bilingual menu folder is huge as variety abounds at every stage, be it morning pastries, Llyn cheddar and pesto sandwiches, light lunchtime salads, simple pasta and pizza meals, or a choice of Welsh ice creams on the day menu. Naturally, good Welsh ingredients are everywhere, especially on the set menu of the day and the evening carte. Braised local lamb shank is served with a mint wine sauce, free-range pork is simply roasted and Bodewyddan venison is slow cooked with sweet paprika and cream. Round off with home-made chocolate torte with apricot coulis, or a platter of superb Welsh cheeses.

Owners: Deiniol ap Dafydd & Chandra Dafydd  Chef: Gwenda Evans
Open: Wed – Sun L 11.00 – 5.00 Wed – Sat D 5.00 – 8.30
Closed: Christmas Day/Boxing Day/New Years Day & 1st week of Jan
Seats: 120 L £12 D £19 10-70
Visa/Mastercard/Switch/Delta  Map reference

# Old Rectory

**Llanrwst Road, Llansanffraid Glan Conwy, Conwy LL28 5LF**
**Tel: 01492 580611**
**Email: info@oldrectorycountryhouse.co.uk**
**www.oldrectorycountryhouse.co.uk**

On A470, 1/2 mile South of its junction with A55

The Georgian-style rectory is set high on a hill overlooking the Conwy estuary and, at night, a floodlit Conwy Castle. Much of the appeal is due to some great food built around the format of a daily changing, no choice fixed-price menu (likes and dislikes are discussed when booking). The country house style incorporates native ingredients which work well in a realistic repertoire that begins in the panelled sitting room with drinks and canapés, followed at table by an amuse bouche, say a demi-tasse of cauliflower and mustard soup and first-rate bread. Fillet of brill with sweet potato and wilted greens with a fig and lemon compote could come next, then roast breast of Gressingham duck, braised Savoy cabbage, black eyed beans and hasselback potato with a port fig jam, whilst choice is reserved for the end – Welsh and Celtic farm cheeses, ice cream, sorbets, or assiette of dessert. Then back to the sitting room for a full-throttle coffee pot and home-made chocolate. As for the wine list, range and quality are evident, prices fair, and there's a good selection of halves.

Owners: Michael & Wendy Vaughan Chefs: Wendy Vaughan & Chris Jones Open: Tues – Sun D only (booking essential) 7.30 for 8.00 Closed: 15th Dec – 1st Jan Seats: 14 D £39.90

Visa/Mastercard/Switch/Delta Map reference 87

**Llansteffan, Carmarthenshire SA33 5JY**
**Tel: 01267 241656**
From Carmarthen, halfway through Llansteffan, on right

Yr Hen Dafarn
Llansteffan

If your idea of restaurant dining includes any notions of prissiness or fuss then this is not the place for you. If, however, your pleasure is bold, gutsy food, simply served (in quantity) then you are in for a treat. Owner Bill Hill has a lot in common with his food; larger than life and unashamedly hedonistic; his character defines his cuisine. This simply furnished old tavern stands at the centre of the seaside village of Llansteffan. Bill has a real hunter-gatherer spirit and chances are he will have had a hand in growing, shooting or catching something on the menu the night you visit. The menu itself is somewhat redundant – far better to talk over the options with Bill or his wife Judith who looks after the dining room. Start perhaps with locally gathered cockles simply cooked in a marinière style with laverbread and old fashioned farmhouse bacon. Fish is always a great bet here and, if you are lucky, Bill may have lobster available served simply with a pot of wobbly mayonnaise, garden fresh salad and an abundance of vegetables. Desserts tend towards the homely and comforting, there may be a crumble or other hot pudding with custard or ice cream. The wine list is short but well chosen.

**L**

Owners: William Hill & Judith Baum  Chef: William Hill
Open: L by prior arrangement (8 plus) D Fri – Sun 6.30 – 9.00, other days by arrangement (8 plus) Seats: 30  L £20 D £20

No Credit Cards  Map reference **88**

# Llansantffraed Court

**Llanvihangel Gobion,
Near Abergavenny NP7 9BA
Tel: 01873 840678
Email: diningout@llch.co.uk
www.llch.co.uk**
From the roundabout at the joining of the A40 & A465 at Abergavenny, follow B4598 for about 5 miles

Drive past the tiny church of St Bride through the mature parkland to Llansantffraed Court: a William and Mary style red brick mansion the majority of which dates back to the early 20th century (make time to explore the grounds with their mature woodland and lake). New chef Simon King cooks in a confident, technically adept style utilising fine ingredients with deftness and taste. The dining room, with its crisp white table linen and period beamed ceiling – in what remains of the original manor house – is intimate yet bright and airy. Impressive culinary skills are demonstrated in dishes such as freshwater crayfish in an open lasagne with silky smooth pasta or perhaps served in a salad with orange, sun-dried tomato and spring onion. Main courses may feature locally sourced rare breed meats such as Gloucester Old Spot pork served in three ways; tender braised belly, roast loin and black pudding. Comforting puddings may include classic dishes such as an unctuous chocolate brownie with chocolate sauce and a tuile basket of vanilla ice cream. Service is willing and well informed. The wine list features around 50 well chosen bins and offers good value for money.

Owner: Mike Morgan  Chef: Simon King  Open: all week
L 12.00 – 2.00  D 7.00 – 8.45  Seats: 60   L £16.50  D £29.50
400   21

C  Visa/Mastercard/Amex/Diners/Switch/Delta   Map reference 89

**Llanwddyn, Powys SY10 0LY**
**Tel: 01691 870692**
Email: res@lakevyrnwy.com
www.lakevyrnwy.com

Drive past Lake Vyrnwy dam on the right hand side of lake, hotel is on the right

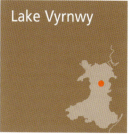

Plenty of wildlife, good fishing and walking and impressive views over Lake Vyrnwy are all part of the allure of this middle-of-nowhere former hunting lodge – the sense of seclusion as the sun sets is powerful. A short, fixed-price dinner menu combines Anglo-French ideas with some more far-flung flavours and there is obvious ambition (although this is not always fully realised). Among the mix-and-match ideas might be terrine of chicken and fennel accompanied by Moroccan couscous with oils and vinegar, as well as pan-seared breast of pigeon with sweet potato purée on a cassoulet of beans and lentils. Main courses centre on roast rack of Lake Vyrnwy lamb with fondant potato and garlic, ratatouille and thyme jus, or pan-roasted breast of duck with dauphinoise potato and sweet onion jus. Seafood may turn up as pan-fried crispy cod with white bean, chorizo and tomato ragout, confit plum tomato, braised fennel and basil pesto. Desserts feature the likes of apple mousse with vanilla froth and orange sorbet or a hot chocolate fondant with white peach ice cream. House wines range from £14.95 to £18.50.

Owner: Marketglen Ltd Chef: Tony Gudgen Open: all week
L 12.00 – 2.00 D 7.00 – 9.15 Closed: 1 week in Feb
Seats: 90 L £12.50 D £32.50
120 35
Visa/Mastercard/Amex/Diners/Switch/Delta Map reference 90

# Carlton House

**Dôl-y-coed Road, Llanwrtyd Wells, Powys LD5 4RA**
**Tel: 01591 610248**
**Email: info@carltonrestaurant.co.uk**
**www.carltonrestaurant.co.uk**
Centre of town opposite the family butcher

True Taste hospitality 2004-5

True Taste hospitality Bronze 2003-4

True Taste hospitality Silver 2002-3

Alan and Mary Ann Gilchrist's handsome Edwardian house is set in one of the remotest parts of Powys in wonderful hiking country, but the warm personal style and short choice dinners make it more than just a handy base for walkers. The style is an individual one. Mary Ann cooks what she likes, following her nose rather than any particular school. Meals have begun with a trio of Welsh cured meats with rocket, celeriac remoulade, Parmesan cheese and a balsamic vinegar dressing, while richer first courses have included a classic avocado pear with fresh crab mayonnaise. Nothing superfluous is added to dishes, roast rack of local spring lamb with herbed couscous, roast Mediterranean vegetables and salsa verde is a wonderfully cohesive dish thanks to fine ingredients simply cooked in perfect balance. Game and fish are both extremely well handled, with Welsh venison teamed with smoky mash and buttered cabbage, while ragout of Cardigan Bay seafood impresses by its freshness. Dishes may appear simple and unfussy, but they embody considerable skill, not least amongst desserts like fresh raspberry pavlova with elderflower syllabub. Prices are reasonable and half bottles plentiful on a thoughtfully constructed wine list.

Owners: Alan & Mary Ann Gilchrist  Chef: Mary Ann Gilchrist
Open: L Tues – Fri 12.00 – 1.30  D Mon – Sat 7.00 – 8.30
Closed: 10th – 30th Dec  Seats: 16  L £25  D £38

Visa/Mastercard/Switch/Delta  Map reference 91

**The Square, Llanwrtyd Wells,
Powys LD5 4RA**
Tel: 01591 610264
Email: foodfoodfood@lycos.com
www.food-food-food.co.uk
Centre of Llanwrtyd Wells

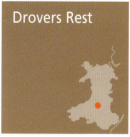

## Drovers Rest

## Llanwrtyd Wells

At first glance, Peter James' stone-built restaurant beside the bridge over the River Irfon resembles a traditional tea shop with its bric-à-brac, cakes on display and homely welcome – but there's much more. The casual daytime bistro atmosphere encourages dropping in for a snack or informal lunch as well as cakes. The printed menu lists the more enduring items – fishcakes, salads, pasta, grilled sirloin steak, lamb and leek curry – while a blackboard chips in with today's soup, the market's fish and any seasonal or local opportunities (grilled gammon steak served with eggs and tomato, for example, comes from locally bred Modern Welsh pigs). In the evening candles are lit and a broader brush is applied, producing red snapper with lemon and ginger, Brecon venison in red wine, or duck breast glazed with Welsh honey with orange and cointreau sauce. A special fish menu is offered every Friday. Puddings such as tiramisu or black cherry meringue roulade are made by Paulette Reed, mother of first chef Stuart. Welsh wines figure on a list that opens at £9.50 and keeps below £15.

True Taste
hospitality
Bronze 2003-4

Owner: Peter R James   Chefs: Stuart J Reed & P Reed
Open: Tues – Sun L 11.30 – 2.30 D 7.30 – 9.30   Closed: Christmas Day
Seats: 40  L £15 D £22.50

**C** Visa/Mastercard/Amex/Diners/Switch/Delta   Map reference

# Lasswade Country House

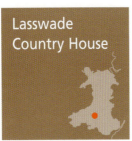

Station Road, Llanwrtyd Wells,
Powys LD5 4RW
Tel: 01591 610515
Email: info@lasswadehotel.co.uk
www.lasswadehotel.co.uk

Roger and Emma Stevens smart Edwardian house in addition to being a fine restaurant and hotel is very much the family home and patrons are treated very much as welcome house guests rather than simply paying customers. Whilst Emma tends to look after diners and Roger devotes his time to the kitchen either is likely to take orders or wait on tables. Roger has enjoyed a distinguished career in some of London's finest hotels and his confident, assured cookery is straightforward and to the point. Tasty starters may include an accomplished sweet red onion and goats' cheese tartlet or perhaps terrine of duck confit. Produce is carefully sourced and Roger has developed a good relationship with local suppliers of meats and fish. Pork may come, with a nod to the Balkans, as roast loin rubbed with garlic and paprika; local Welsh Lamb and beef also feature prominently. The dining room with its sparkling glassware and polished tables has an air of elegant formality but service itself is far from stuffy. Tasty puddings may include a cognac scented crème brûlée or perhaps crisp apple strudel with ice cream. The wine list is carefully constructed and offers good value for money.

Owner: Roger Stevens Chef: Roger Stevens Open: all week D only 7.30 – 9.00 Closed: Christmas Day Seats: 20 D £26.50

25/30  8  Visa/Mastercard/Switch/Delta  Map reference 93

**Llyswen, Brecon, Powys LD3 0YP**
**Tel: 01874 754525**
**Email: enquiries@llangoedhall.com**
**www.llangoedhall.com**
On the A470, 9 miles from Builth Wells and 10 miles from Brecon

This Jacobean manor house designed by Clough Williams-Ellis of Portmeirion fame is intended to offer a classic country house party experience. Featuring fabrics and furnishings from owner Sir Bernard Ashley's on site Elanbach label: the house is the epitome of elegant country living. Food continues in the same traditional country house vein and new chef Sean Ballington is a master of the style. Starters may include a sinfully rich mousse of salmon and crab liberally stuffed with caviar and served with punchy Gower crab bisque. Carefully sourced ingredients may include breast of free-range guinea fowl which comes with leek mash and a earthy cep cream sauce. The temptation continues at pudding with wickedly boozy griottine cherries accompanied by an accurate white and dark chocolate mousse – a heady example of the style. Staff are well drilled in the niceties of formal dining with the rituals of wine service being particularly carefully observed. The wine list starts pricey and rapidly heads towards the stratosphere, but diners have the opportunity to choose many rare vintages which are unlikely to be seen elsewhere.

Owner: Sir Bernard Ashley Chef: Sean Ballington Open: all week
L 12.00 – 2.00 D 7.00 – 9.00 Seats: 30  L £28.50 D £43
60  23  P  V  r
C  Visa/Mastercard/Amex/Diners/Switch/Delta  Map reference  94

## Wynnstay

*Machynlleth*

**Maengwyn Street, Machynlleth,
Powys SY20 8AE
Tel: 01654 702941
Email: info@wynnstay-hotel.com**
In centre of town, opposite clock tower

Beneath the fluttering red and yellow banners of Owain Glyndŵr in his ancient capital, this long established hotel strikes a stylish balance of the modern and the classical. The restaurant combines contemporary colours and styling with period furnishings and as such has it's finger on the pulse in terms of modern restaurant design. Chef Gareth Johns fine cuisine also owes a lot to this philosophy. He ably updates classic dishes and reworks them for the modern appetite. Start, perhaps, with excellent crab cakes served with a modish lemon scented couscous or pigeon and chicken terrine with a tomato and onion chutney. Meats frequently come from local Dyfi valley suppliers and are of excellent quality. Lamb may feature as roast rump with lentil gravy, colcannon and crisp green beans or fillet of Welsh Black beef may be sautéed with a cracked pepper sauce, new potatoes and sauté courgettes. Puddings tend to be similarly classical in style with old favourites such as lemon tart or dark chocolate fondant with damson sorbet dominating the puddings list. The wine list is very well selected and in particular there is a superb range of interesting Italian bottles.

Owners: Charles & Sheila Dark  Chef: Gareth Johns  Open: all week
L 12.00 – 2.00 D 6.30 – 9.00  Closed: Christmas Day Eve  Seats: 50
🍽 L £15 D £27

🛏23 P ♿ V 🎋 ❀ ✕ 🍴 📶

C  Visa/Mastercard/Amex/Diners/Switch/Delta   Map reference  **95**

**Eglwys Fach, Machynlleth, SY20 8TA**
Tel: 01654 781209
Email: info@ynyshir-hall.co.uk
www.ynyshir-hall.co.uk
On the A487, 5.5 miles South of Machynlleth

One of the finest hotels in Wales, Ynyshir Hall, a member of the prestigious consortium Relais et Chateaux, epitomises all that is good about staying in a country house. Acres of pristine parkland surround the elegant house and levels of comfort throughout are exceptional. Hosts Joan and Rob Reen take great pride in looking after their guests and their well drilled staff are professional and charming. Take drinks and canapés in the bar or drawing room before sitting down to the accomplished and precise cuisine of new chef Adam Simmonds. Begin, perhaps, with a delicate starter of carefully sourced langoustines and plump oysters simply poached and served with a fragrant seafood broth. Main courses see the use of great ingredients such as tender salt marsh lamb slowly cooked at a low temperature to maintain succulence or poached fillet of beef with a modish horseradish foam. Precisely crafted puddings may include a contemporary reworking of old classics like reconstructed 'rhubarb and custard'. The wine list has been compiled with care and thought and offers an exceptional selection of vintages and many carefully sourced half bottles.

True Taste hospitality Gold 2003-4

Owners: Joan & Rob Reen  Chef: Adam Simmonds  Open: all week
L 12.30 – 1.30  D 7.00 – 8.45  Closed: 3 weeks in January  Seats: 30
L £29.50  D £49
15  9
Visa/Mastercard/Amex/Diners/Switch/Delta  Map reference  96

## Mold

### Glasfryn

**Raikes Lane, Sychdyn, Mold, Denbighshire CH7 6LR**
Tel: 01352 750500
Email: glasfryn@brunningandprice.co.uk
www.glasfryn-mold.co.uk
Near the Theatre Clwyd

Standing opposite Theatr Clwyd, this striking red brick former farmhouse is the second Welsh venture across the border for the upmarket pub group Brunning & Price. Looking out across rolling countryside, Glasfryn is the bright, noisy London-style 'gastropub' that North Wales has long been waiting for. Here, theatre-goers are part of a lively crowd that come to eat as much or as little as they want at large scrubbed tables in the warren of spacious and tastefully decorated rooms. There's no music, but with bare board floors, high ceilings and crowds at the big, oak-panelled bar, a cheerful buzz fills the place, which extends out onto the bench-filled front terrace on fine summer evenings. Food is modern 'pub grub' and well above average for the area. Available all day everyday, daily menus may take in polenta fried tiger prawns with mango and pepper salsa for starters, followed by a generous braised shoulder of lamb with red cabbage, roast potatoes and honey and rosemary sauce, or traditional Cumberland sausage with mash and onion gravy. Puddings include sticky toffee pudding with vanilla ice cream. You can order sandwiches in the evening and you'll find six real ales on tap and a raft of reasonably priced wines by the glass.

Owners: Jerry Brunning & Graham Price  Chef: Tim Watts
Open: all week 12.00 – 9.30  Closed: Christmas Day/Boxing Day
Seats: 200  L £19  D £19

Visa/Mastercard/Amex/Switch/Delta   Map reference **97**

7 Church Street, Monmouth,
Monmouthshire NP25 3BX
Tel: 01600 712600
Email:
bob@bobsmonmouth.freeserve.co.uk
Fourth up Church Street, on the left,
50 yards from Agincourt Square

# Bobs

Monmouth

Pedestrianised Church Street is a haven of peace away from the high street hustle and bustle. Occupying a prime position, with a chalked-up easel board outside enticing you in for bargain two-course lunches, is this rather off-the-wall café-come-restaurant. Beyond the old artefacts and general clutter that fills the window you will find a long narrow room with informal café-style seating leading through to a tiny bar and a rear restaurant. Old metal signs and wine box ends line the walls and old pots, jugs and bric-a-brac hang from the beams. Informality reigns supreme, so call in for morning coffee or just a pot of tea, or come for lunch, the 'bits and bobs' menu on the table listing an array of pasta meals, salads and imaginative sandwiches. Look to the menu boards for the give-away two course lunch, perhaps curried squash soup followed by baked cod with tomato and basil, the equally cheap early bird supper menu, or splash out and order from the carte – plump scallops pan-fried with beans, pancetta and mango, followed by sirloin steak with pepper sauce and banoffee pie for instance.

**M**

Owner: Bob Evans Chef: Richard Lamass Open: Tues – Sat
L 12.00 – 2.00 D 6.00 – 9.45 Closed: 2 weeks middle of Feb & Oct,
3 days Christmas Seats: 60 🍽 L £15 D £25

C Visa/Mastercard/Switch/Delta  Map reference  98

**698 Mumbles Road, Mumbles,
Swansea SA3 4EH
Tel: 01792 361616
Email: info@698.uk.com
www.698.uk.com**
Halfway between Oystermouth Square
and Mumbles Pier

True Taste
hospitality
2004-5

Sam Thomas is not a chef to hide his light under a bushel and is clearly comfortable with opening his kitchen to scrutiny, working as he does behind a glass viewing screen. With one year behind them the partners at 698 are already gaining a considerable reputation locally for serving some of the most accurate and sophisticated cuisine along the seafront. Striking contemporary décor with high end details such as high-class glassware and china indicate that this is a restaurant of serious intent. The restaurant offers a range of modern European dishes which are prepared with real care and garnished without fuss or frippery. Lunchtime can be a real bargain with three courses available for under £15 a head which for cooking of this quality is something of a steal. Starters typical of the style could be a risotto of confit rabbit and porcini mushroom or spaghetti with shrimp and pesto. Peasant classics like confit of duck leg with paysanne potatoes sit well with the luxury of locally caught sea bass with rocket mash and piquant salsa verde. The great front of house staff are keen, attentive and sensitive to their customers' needs.

Owners: Alison Fisher & Sam Thomas  Chef: Sam Thomas
Open: Tues – Sun L 12.30 – 2.30 D 6.30 – 9.30
Closed: first 2 weeks Jan  Seats 38-40  L £12.95 D £28

Visa/Mastercard/Amex/Switch/Delta   Map reference **99**

**93 Newton Road, Mumbles,
Swansea SA3 4BN
Tel: 01792 366006
Email: info@claudes.org.uk
www.claudes.org.uk**
At the top end of Newton Road, in Mumbles village

Mumbles

Andrew and Penny Lauder's charming restaurant touches all the right bases and with four years under their belts both cooking and service have very much come of age. Andrew's food is contemporary in style and unfussy. He lets ingredients speak for themselves and is unconcerned with frivolous garnishes and the dictates of fashion. This kitchen is perfectly capable of producing dishes which demand high levels of culinary technique as demonstrated in an accurately cooked crab risotto with well-timed pan fried diver caught scallops. Local beef and lamb feature strongly and may appear in such dishes as fillet of Welsh Black beef with red cabbage and potato gratin. Be sure to leave room for pudding or cheese, guests are offered a selection of four cheeses from a list of around 8 – 10 and these can include Perl Wen or Caws Llyn as well and some other British and French classics. The carte offers about 10 main dishes but budget conscious guests will appreciate the set dinner menu offering three courses for less than £20. With a handful of wines available by the glass and a 50 bin list once again you may well feel spoiled for choice.

M

Owners: Andrew & Penny Lauder  Chef: Andrew Lauder
Open: L all week 12.00 – 2.30  D Mon – Sat 6.30 – 9.30
Closed: Boxing Day to Jan 2nd  Seats: 60   L £11  D £17
👥 40  P  ♿ V  🚹 ✕ ✂
C  Visa/Mastercard/Amex/Diners/Switch/Delta  Map reference 100

129

## Fredericks

Mumbles

**Carlton Hotel, 654 – 656 Mumbles Road, Mumbles, Swansea SA3 4EA**
**Tel: 01792 368900**
**Email: mail@carltonmumbles.co.uk**
**www.carltonmumbles.co.uk**
Opposite the car park, in between the village and the pier

This slick restaurant boasts a safe pair of hands at the culinary helm with chef Frederick Pallade continuing to impress with his skilful take on Franco-Welsh cuisine. His food is firmly rooted in the classical tradition, but is also evolved and thoroughly up to date in style. Dishes like an impressively fresh seafood open ravioli starter, with silky pasta, plump cockles and sauce vierge, serve to highlight the work of a chef who knows how to combine great local produce with carefully honed technique. Similarly, dishes like poussin perfumed with lemon and tarragon stand as a great example of doing the simple things well. Waiting staff work hard to stay up to speed with the kitchens efforts, but there can be occasional hiccups in service. A relatively short selection of desserts might worry the sweet toothed, but when one of the puddings offered is as assured as a creamy smooth white chocolate torte perfumed with lavender then the lack of choice seems much less important. The concise wine list features 38 bins with a couple available by the glass.

Owner: Kevin Rees Chef: Frederick Pallade Open: Tues – Sat
L 12.00 – 2.30 D 7.00 – 9.30 Closed: Christmas Day Seats: 32
L £13.95 D £25
20
Visa/Mastercard/Amex/Diners/Switch/Delta  Map reference **101**

**614 – 616 Mumbles Road,
Mumbles, Swansea SA3 4EA
Tel: 01792 363184**
On Mumbles sea front

Michael Knight is perhaps the most experimental chef working on the famous Mumbles Mile. His cuisine draws on influences from across the globe and whilst labelling the cooking as 'fusion food' would be rather too prescriptive, it serves as an indication of what is on offer here. Whilst there is no fear of drawing on influences from far and wide, it's when restraint is shown that the dishes tend to shine all the brighter. A starter of crab spring roll with zesty coriander and a sweet and sour sauce is fairly typical of the style. Impressive technical skills are on show with a carefully boned and stuffed saddle of rabbit being strong evidence of a commitment to getting the basic techniques right. Puddings tend to be more traditional in style and are all the more effective because of this. The room is bright and modern and showcases a collection of striking glassware, with an appropriate seaside theme to the décor and bold primary colours are used to great effect. Staff too are bright, very well informed and cheerful. The wine list shows care in its compilation and offers vintages to suit all pockets.

Owner: Michael Knight Chef: Michael Knight Open: Tues – Sun
L 12.00 – 2.30 D 6.30 – 9.30 Closed: Christmas Day/Boxing Day/
New Years Day Seats: 90 L £12.50 D £25

Visa/Mastercard/Amex/Diners/Switch/Delta  Map reference

# Mermaid

**686 Mumbles Road,
Mumbles, Swansea SA3 4EE
Tel: 01792 367744**

Along the Mumbles Road, a large red brick building on the right

Having achieved much at Chelsea Café in Swansea, the move to brand new (and considerably larger) premises in Mumbles sees the start of a new chapter in Nick Bevan's professional life. Styled as a restaurant and coffee lounge this establishment is open all day for drinks, light meals and the impressive restaurant offering. Stripped wood floors, eau de nil walls and art deco accents, coupled with an impressive view over Swansea Bay, make this a great dining destination. Nick Bevan is known for having a deft hand with locally sourced seafood and his dedication to procuring the freshest doesn't falter. Starters include a signature dish of seafood broth (more a cream soup than a traditional broth) with a French style casserole of seafood and shellfish and rouille crouton. Well informed waiting staff are happy to recommend what's best from the market each day and it is certainly worth paying attention to the list of specials. Carnivores are not, however, neglected with carefully prepared Welsh Black beef and salt marsh lamb also featuring strongly on the menu. The concise wine list does well to list many less familiar bins and certainly rewards those with the desire to explore less traditional regions.

Owners: Lisa & Nicholas Bevan Chef: Nicholas Bevan Open: all week L 12.00 – 2.30 Tues – Sat D 7.00 – 9.30 Closed: Christmas Day/Boxing Day Seats: 112 L £13.50 D £18

Visa/Mastercard/Amex/Switch/Delta  Map reference **103**

**Norton Road, Mumbles,
Swansea SA3 5TQ
Tel: 01792 404891
Email: nortonhouse@btconnect.com**
www.nortonhousehotel.co.uk
On A4067 Swansea to Mumbles Road, 1 mile after 'Welcome to Mumbles' sign, turn right into Norton Road

Mumbles

A haven from the bustle of the nearby Mumbles Mile, Norton House is a real family hotel owned for many years by Jan and John Power. They are ably assisted by son Mark who clearly enjoys his 'mine host' duties. This hotel is a great example of traditional hotel keeping done well with, for example, synchronised silver cloche lifting being a hallmark of restaurant service here. Enjoy an aperitif in the cosy bar before being escorted through to the high ceilinged dining room with polished wood tables and crisp linen napkins. Chef Mark Comisini makes good use of local ingredients and diners can expect such dishes as fillet of Welsh Black beef perhaps accompanied by a Caerphilly cheese, leek and potato cake or local asparagus in a salad with rocket, Parmesan and pesto. Carefully constructed puddings could include chocolate torte with coconut and walnut. A young well trained team looks after the dining room and have ready smiles for their guests. The wine list holds lots of interest and is good value for money.

**M**

Owners: C J & J Power Chef: Mark Comisini Open: all week D only 7.00 – 9.30 Closed: 1 week at Christmas Seats: 46 D £28.50
24 15 P V r
C Visa/Mastercard/Amex/Diners/Switch/Delta Map reference

# Patricks with Rooms

**638 Mumbles Road, Mumbles, Swansea SA3 4EA**
**Tel: 01792 360199**
**www.patrickswithrooms.com**
From Swansea, keep sea on your left through Mumbles, Patricks is on the right

Located at the heart of the Mumbles Mile, Patricks has been a real success story over the years, expanding into neighbouring premises and adding eight stylish contemporary bedrooms. The restaurant with its green gingham tablecloths and view over Swansea Bay remains the heart of the business. Patrick Walsh and Dean Fuller offer an eclectic menu and are unafraid to draw inspiration from all over the globe. Local ingredients feature in dishes like seafood risotto with smoked salmon and salt marsh lamb with a pesto and parmesan crust. There are sometimes ambitious flavour combinations, and it's when natural bedfellows are allowed to combine, as in a rich chocolate mocha cup with a chocolate chip cookie 'for dunking', that the cuisine tends to speak most clearly. Guests enjoy a wide selection of menu choices and these are supplemented with a range of value for money blackboard specials. Catherine Walsh runs front of house with an eye for detail and her staff are well drilled and friendly. Diners' wallets will enjoy the brief but sensibly priced wine list which features many familiar bins, with a number available by the glass.

Owners: Catherine & Patrick Walsh/Sally & Dean Fuller
Chefs: Patrick Walsh & Dean Fuller Open: L all week 12.00 – 2.20 D Mon – Sat 6.30 – 9.50 Closed: 3 weeks Sept, 1 week Jan, Christmas Day/Boxing Day Seats: 75 L £18 D £35 8

Visa/Mastercard/Amex/Switch/Delta Map reference 105

**Nant-y-Derry, Monmouthshire NP7 9DN**
**Tel: 01873 881101**
Email: info@thefoxhunter.com
www.thefoxhunter.com
Between Usk and Abergavenny, off the A4042

Foxhunter

Nant-y-Derry

**N**

It's always a pleasure when somewhere new and exciting bursts onto the eating out scene in Wales and makes an impact well beyond the country's borders. This was formerly a station master's house, but is now a contemporary dining room and small bar that has managed to pull off the trick of being stylish but also relaxed. These are adjectives which pretty much sum up the food too. There is nothing too fussy about the cooking which is centred on Italian regional cuisine but it's done with an understanding and care rarely seen. The omens are good from the moment you're presented with excellent focaccia and ciabatta. Deceptively straightforward dishes like pizetta bianca (a wonderfully crisp pizza base with thin slices of potato, mozzarella and truffle) and a gently curried seafood stew are beautifully handled. Sourcing of ingredients is clearly a passion and it shows in fresh lasagne with cep sauce and a gorgeous piece of wild bass with brown shrimps and couscous and satisfying puddings may feature seasonal crumbles or a rice pudding with summer berries. The wine list is packed with character and should leave you spoilt for choice.

**Owners:** Matt & Lisa Tebbutt **Chef:** Matt Tebbutt **Open:** Tues – Sat L 12.00 – 2.30 D 7.00 – 10.00 **Closed:** Christmas/New Years Day, 2 weeks in Feb **Seats:** 60 L £22 D £26

60 P

Visa/Mastercard/Switch/Delta  Map reference

# Chandlery

77 – 78 Lower Dock Street,
Newport NP20 1EH
Tel: 01633 256622
www.chandleryrestaurant.co.uk
On the A48 at the foot of George Street bridge

Take the A48 into Newport and you won't be able to miss the Chandlery as it appears brightly before you on the outskirts of the city centre. It's an appealing Georgian building that looks exceptionally smart on the outside and just as crisp within, where the dining areas occupy two floors. The interior is stylish and understated and it's a pattern reflected in the menu with a selection of simply described dishes based on good quality, often local ingredients. A starter of lobster salad typifies the approach being a combination of sweet lobster meat presented with some fresh asparagus, avocado and soft quail's eggs. Dishes can be triumphantly uncomplicated, as in sea bass with hand-cut chips and tartare sauce or more sophisticated (and perhaps a little less successful) in a trio of salt marsh lamb comprising roast rump, pan fried liver and a torte of shoulder. Desserts are handled with some skill and might include a generous raspberry and lemon version of the much underrated trifle or a chocolate fondant with white chocolate mousse. Staff are exceptionally well-drilled and really eager to please. A wine list of sensible length is good value and jam packed with character.

Owners: Simon & Jane Newcombe  Chef: Simon Newcombe
Open: L Tues – Friday 12.00 – 2.00  D Tues – Sat 7.00 – 10.00
Closed: 1 week at Christmas  Seats: 70  L £12.95  D £25

45

Visa/Mastercard/Amex/Switch/Delta  Map reference 107

**Station Approach, Bassaleg,
Newport NP10 8LD
Tel: 01633 891891
Email: enquiries@junction28.com
www.junction28.com**
Off junction 28 of the M4

Junction 28 may not be quite adjacent to the M4 interchange of the same name, but its close proximity and the fact that it is housed in a former railway station are more than enough to justify the clever moniker. Perhaps a little of its bustling trade can be accounted for by those seeking refuge from the offerings of motorway service stations but much of it is clearly down to having quickly built up a loyal following of more local custom.
A large à la carte menu takes in a range of cooking styles with dishes that run from tempura of prawns through Mediterranean crab strudel, to a classic best end of lamb with boulangère potatoes. This is honest, enjoyable cooking that might not always be of pinpoint accuracy but can be relied upon to offer bright, generous flavours and the regularly changing daily menu is something of a bargain. The wine list covers most bases and offers some good value of its own, particularly in France. A genial team of staff cope well with the large venue which was about to undergo refurbishment at the time of our visit.

Owners: Jon West & Richard Wallace Chef: Jean-Jacques Payel Open: L all week 12.00 – 2.00 (12.00 – 4.00 Sun) D Mon – Sat 5.30 – 9.30 Closed: Boxing Day/New Years Day Seats: 165 L £12.45 D £13.95

100

Visa/Mastercard/Amex/Switch/Delta  Map reference

## Owens

**Coldra Woods, Newport NP18 1HQ**
**Tel: 01633 410342**
**Email:**
**restaurantbookings@celtic-manor.com**
**www.celtic-manor.com**
Off the M4, at Junction 24

The Celtic Manor Resort Hotel is a striking sight, dominating the hillside above the M4. The lower floors of the hotel are superbly geared towards large conferences and the wide ranging leisure facilities include championship golf courses, swimming pool and gymnasium. Owens, the hotel's fine dining restaurant is tucked away and subdued, the restaurant is run by a young, enthusiastic team and service is professional and sometimes a touch over-attentive. The fixed price menu features a wide range of local produce used in imaginative and ambitious dishes, Gower scallops, sewin, Raglan pork and Welsh cheeses are all put to good use. Typical of the style is an enterprising assembly centring on a slow-roasted fillet of beef with braised rib meat, confit of garlic and a modish horseradish foam.
In similar vein chunky fillets of sea bass are outlandishly paired with cep stuffed chicken wings and a roast chicken sauce. Desserts are elaborate and extravagantly presented in combinations such as pear and blackberry jelly with pear and goats' cheese wonton, pear sorbet and pear frangipane tart. The wine list is a much improved document but doesn't show much restraint in terms of mark-up.

Owner: Sir Terence Mathews  Chef: Nicholas Evans  Open: Mon – Sat D only 7.00 – 10.00 (10.30 Fri – Sat) Closed: Bank Holiday Mondays Seats: 50 D £45

440 P r

Visa/Mastercard/Amex/Diners/Switch/Delta  Map reference 109

**East Street, Newport,
Pembrokeshire SA42 0SY
Tel: 01239 820575**
Email: cnapan@online-holidays.net
www.online-holidays.net/cnapan
Centre of Newport on
Fishguard/Cardigan road

Cnapan

Newport (Pembrokeshire)

**N**

Cnapan is one of those wonderful places that has done a sterling job for eating out in Wales over a period of many years. On visiting, it's apparent that those involved have been in this game for some time. The smiling and well-organised service, the absence of serious delays on the busiest nights and the sheer consistency of the cooking, all tell you that this is a well-practised operation. This is not a place that follows fads, the interior has the look of a charming home, which is essentially what it is and the food is notable for it's accurate cooking, seasoning and the quality of the ingredients. Nobody should complain about that. A perfectly cooked piece of fish is too rare a find but you may get it here in the form of a plump piece of hake served with a watercress sauce taken from a daily board of fish dishes. There are plenty of meat options too such as breast of duck with a bitter orange glaze or marinated pork with a coriander, pineapple and cranberry salsa. Desserts, like a satisfying chocolate 'crunch' with pistachio and sour cherries, are a highlight. A neat well-chosen wine list has some good French regional bins.

Owners: Michael & Judith Cooper, John & Eluned Lloyd Chef: Judith Cooper Open: Mon, Wed – Sat L 12.00 – 2.00 Wed – Mon D 6.45 – 8.45 Closed: Christmas Day/Boxing Day/Jan & Feb
Seats: 36 L £12.50 D £27.50 5
C Visa/Mastercard/Switch/Delta Map reference 110

# Old Radnor

## Harp Inn

**Old Radnor, Near Prestigne, Powys LD8 2RH**
**Tel: 01544 350655**

Take A44 from Kington to Rhayader, in Walton, turn left for Old Radnor

This and the church of St Stephen (take time to view the rare medieval altar screen) are practically all there is to this tiny hamlet. The Radnor Valley and Radnor Forest provide energetic diversion for walkers and Erfyl Protheroe offers welcome restoration in his 15th century inn which consists of two interlinked slate-floored bars sporting beams, ancient settles with a log fire, and a pretty buttermilk dining room with polished floorboards and well-spaced tables. An unpretentious atmosphere is created by a cheerful absence of formality in the front of house approach and by the four square cooking of Heather Price. The formula is a blackboard menu with a wholesome approach that deals in raw materials from mainly local suppliers. The short repertoire embraces grilled Hereford rump steak with pepper sauce or 18oz battered cod with proper chips and although precision may not be the strongest suit, a first-course garlic and ginger creel prawns, accurately cooked vegetables with fillet of trout with a pesto crumble and pesto sauce and a benchmark Bakewell tart for dessert will suit many down to the ground. Drink Timothy Taylor Landlord or choose from the short Tanners list, which starts with Chilean house wine at £9.75.

Owners: E Protheroe & H M Price  Chefs: E Protheroe & H M Price
Open: L Sat – Sun 12.00 – 2.00  D Tues – Sun D 7.00 – 9.00
Closed: Christmas Day  Seats: 40  L £13  D £16
20  5
Visa/Mastercard/Switch/Delta  Map reference 111

**Rhydycroesau, Oswestry, Shropshire
SY10 7JD
Tel: 01691 653700
Email: stay@peny.co.uk
www.peny.co.uk**
Take B4580 from Oswestry and hotel will be signed, 3 miles from town, on left

This little oasis of calm straddles the English Welsh border in the heart of Shropshire. The former rectory is a pretty building with a naturally warm atmosphere, which is further enhanced by the friendly staff. A two or three course fixed price meal may be ordered from the daily changing menu whilst snuggling infront of the log fire and nibbling the canapés. The dining room has the reassuring feel of another era and service runs like a well-oiled machine. Terrine of rosé veal is marked as 'welfare friendly reared' and is studded with pistachios and apricots and served with an apple chutney, whilst the celery and Yorkshire blue cheese tart with onion marmalade may appeal to the vegetarian diner. A good winter venison casserole with root vegetables and herb couscous is made more fancy by arriving in a filo basket, and grilled pink snapper is well timed and served on home-made tagliolini with pak choi, although the addition of tzatziki is not so successful. The selection of organic cheeses looks an enticing option, served with poached pear, Welsh rarebit and bara brith, and a choice of desserts is also available.

Owners: Audrey & Miles Hunter  Chef: David Morris  Open: all week D only 6.30 – 8.30  Closed: 20th Dec – 25th Jan  Seats: 40  D £28

Visa/Mastercard/Amex/Switch/Delta  Map reference

## Old Kings Arms

13 Main Street, Pembroke,
Pembrokeshire SA71 4JS
Tel: 01646 683611
Email: reception@oldkingsarmshotel.freeserve.co.uk
www.oldkingsarmshotel.co.uk
Situated on Pembroke main street, 200 yards from castle

Bags of old world charm in this pub restaurant: terracotta walls, a big open fireplace, rows of copper pots and a stripped wood floor set a rustic scene befitting a 15th century coaching inn. The restaurant menu includes an impressive selection of fresh local fish and quality ingredients such as Welsh Lamb, tender, flavour-packed corn fed chicken and Pant Mawr cheese – topped with almonds, grilled very lightly and served with sweet red pepper chutney. Expect hearty portions of vegetables such as perfectly timed broccoli, nicely browned potatoes dauphinoise and sauté potatoes. Technical accuracy is good when it comes to cooking meats and vegetables, so the simpler dishes such as pan fried Welsh Black fillet steak with mushrooms should impress. Perhaps be more cautious with the more adventurous sounding dishes, which struggle to bring ingredients such as breast of corn fed chicken with baked banana, sweetcorn and bacon into a cohesive whole. The well-informed wine list runs to over 50 bottles, including plenty of half bottles.

Owner: S E Wheeler Chef: Oliver Wooles Open: all week
L 12.00 – 2.30 D 7.00 – 10.00 Closed: Christmas Day/Boxing Day/New Years Day Seats: 36 L £13.50 D £21

18 P V

Visa/Mastercard/Amex/Switch/Delta   Map reference 113

**46 Plassey Street, Penarth,
Vale of Glamorgan CF64 1EL
Tel: 029 2033 0829/2070 7774
Email: cornerhouse46@ntl.world.com**
Off Windsor Road

## Corner House

*Penarth*

This small streetcorner restaurant is big on atmosphere: think 1920s Paris – Lloyd Loom bistro café chairs, stripped floors and art deco lighting. Smart, friendly staff glide from table to table and a contented buzz of conversation is backed by quiet, Billie Holiday-style Jazz recordings. On one wall, a gargantuan wine rack displays the spoils of the proprietors' wine buying odyssey around France. It's an excellent wine list, with all their discoveries available to take home. The French theme extends to the cooking, which is simple but artful, with plenty of personal touches. Start with the likes of salad foie, moules or a memorable vegetarian option of aubergine grilled and stacked with mushrooms and Welsh cheese, served in a pool of puréed roasted red pepper. Main courses could include fresh and beautifully presented monkfish with a light Parmesan and breadcrumb crust, greens and creamed green capsicum peppers or a pepper coated fillet of beef with a cream sauce. Flavours can be a tad understated, but the cooking is assured, technically accurate and uses very fine ingredients. Don't miss the desserts, which could include the richest chocolate mousse, a heavenly home-made banana and lavender honey ice cream, or an assortment of several.

Owner: John Evans Chef: John Evans Open: L Tues – Sat 12.00 – 2.00
D Tues – Sat 6.45 – 9.30 Closed: 1 week in Feb Seats: 40
🍽 L £12.50 D £15.00

**P** **V** 👶r ✗ 🚭

**C** Visa/Mastercard/Switch/Delta  Map reference 🟠**114**

# Olive Tree

21 Glebe Street, Penarth,
Vale of Glamorgan CF64 1EE
Tel: 029 2070 7077
Email: sandmartfrolics@aol.com
www.the-olive-tree.net

From Cardiff link road, head towards Penarth centre, turn left at St Fagans pub, 100 yards on left

The two Martins responsible for the Olive Tree have a long history in the trade and made their name at Frolics in Southerndown. Their move to a more populated location has begun well and it's already common to find the side street premises packed. The interior is simple and contemporary with striking artwork, blonde wood and crisp table linen. It's a cheerful, upbeat venue that benefits greatly from the personality and attention to detail of the front of house staff. The food is similarly bright and easygoing with plenty of classic French and Mediterranean influences on display. Scallops might arrive in a creamy sauce laced with Noilly Prat, lardons, shallots and lime, fishcakes with lemongrass, ginger and a tomato and red onion salsa. Main courses offer a balanced selection of meats and fish which may feature pork tenderloin with capers, glazed apple and a Calvados sauce. Amongst the desserts a classic lemon tart is typical of the style. The wine list is sensibly not overlong but has real character throughout the list at reasonable prices. The fixed price menu is something of a bargain.

Owners: M J Say & M Dobson Chef: Martin Dobson Open: Sun L (Oct – July) 12.00 – 2.30 Tues – Sat D 6.00 – 9.00 Closed: Bank Holidays and first two weeks of Sept Seats: 36 L £14.75 D £18.50

 (after 9.30)

Visa/Mastercard/Switch/Delta  Map reference 115

**Pant Yr Afon, Penmaenmawr,
Conwy LL34 6AD
Tel: 01492 623820**
On the high street, under the arcade

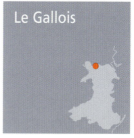

Penmaenmawr clings to the hillside above the busy A55 expressway between Conwy and Bangor and tucked away beneath a Victorian verandah in the main street you will find the unprepossessing slate and bow-windowed façade of this tiny restaurant. The setting may not be grand but Le Gallois is a culinary oasis in these parts. Cheery proprietor Carol Jones and chef-husband Peter have been here 18 years and successfully draw a discerning clientele for Peter's competent modern cooking. What's more, his changing chalkboard menus are sensibly short and feature the best local produce available. At clothed tables in the neat, unpretentious room kick off a satisfying meal with plump and juicy scallops, simply served with a good beurre blanc sauce, or opt for Conwy crab au gratin or the day's freshly made soup, perhaps warming French onion. Best end of local lamb is cooked pink and may be served with a mint and rich Madeira sauce, while turbot fillets are accompanied by a delicious white wine and saffron cream sauce. Rustic dauphinois and al dente broccoli are served on a sizzling skillet with, perhaps, an additional bowl of excellent herby ratatouille. Wines are excellent value with the house selection offered by the glass, carafe and bottle.

Owners: Peter & Carol Jones Chef: Peter Jones Open: Thurs – Sun D only 7.00 – 10.00 Seats: 30 D £20

Visa/Mastercard/Switch/Delta  Map reference

# Penmaenuchaf Hall

**Penmaenpool, Dolgellau, Gwynedd LL40 1YB**
**Tel: 01341 422129**
**Email: relax@penhall.co.uk**
**www.penhall.co.uk**
From the A470, take the A493 towards Tywyn & Fairbourne, Hall is 1 mile on left

Penmaenuchaf Hall is a haven for lovers of country house elegance. Charming, comfortable lounges with deep sofas and fresh flowers set the scene and the Victorian house boasts some superb views overlooking the Mawddach estuary. Meals are served in the oak panelled dining room with its pristine white linen napery and sparkling glassware. Chef Justin Pilkington demonstrates real culinary talent in the dishes he produces and has the rare skill of knowing when to leave well alone. Start, perhaps, with a terrine of pressed duck confit studded with red wine poached pears or sample a classic Gazpacho heady with Mediterranean flavours. Main courses make great use of local produce and Justin is unafraid to use contemporary techniques to enhance his carefully sourced ingredients. A carefully seared fillet of salmon may come with herb crushed potatoes and a cutting edge pea foam. The classics are carefully wrought also; best end of lamb comes with smooth shallot purée and rosemary jus. The wine list touches all the right bases and bottles are carefully selected to offer guests a great range of choice.

Owners: Lorraine Fielding & Mark Watson Chefs: Justin Pilkington, Anthony & Tim Reeve Open: all week L 12.00 – 2.00 D 7.00 – 9.30 (9.00 Sun) Seats: 36 L £17.95 D £32.50

50  14

C Visa/Mastercard/Diners/Switch/Delta  Map reference 117

**Pontdolgoch, Near Caersws SY17 5JE
Tel: 01686 688919
Email: info@talkhouse.co.uk
www.talkhouse.co.uk**
1 mile West of Caersws, on the A470

There may be changes in the kitchen since last year's guide, but this smart roadside dining pub continues to offer a sympathetic mix of drinks in the classic Mytton Bar (or more quietly in the small, separate lounge), then eating off polished wooden tables in the light modern dining room overlooking the garden. It's a comfortable and sophisticated environment for owner Stephen Garrett's Welsh-infused but broadly based blackboard menu, which changes daily. His straightforward bistro style is up to date without attempting anything too outrageous. The appeal is that the food doesn't stray too far from its pubby roots – informality and decent sized portions are among the attractions – and yet is able to produce smooth terrine of pork and Armagnac with onion chutney, and roast pavé of wild pig. Native ingredients are well to the fore, in the form of Carmarthen ham (served as a starter with crotin de chevre and salad), Welsh fillet with shallot rösti and braised salt marsh lamb with dauphinoise potatoes. An exemplar lemon tart makes a perfect finish. There is Tetleys on tap, several wines of the month, and the 85 bin list opens with house wine at £12.

Owners: Stephen & Mark Garratt  Chef: Stephen Garratt
Open: L Wed – Sun 12.00 – 1.45  D Tues – Sat 6.30 – 8.45
Closed: Christmas Day  Seats: 35  L £24  D £26

Visa/Mastercard/Switch/Delta  Map reference 118

## Tregynon Farmhouse

**Ponfaen**

Gwaun Valley, Pontfaen, Near Fishguard, Pembrokeshire SA65 9TU
Tel: 01239 820531
Email: tregynon@online-holidays.net
www.tregynon-cottages.co.uk
At cross roads of B4313/B4329, take B4313 towards Fishguard, take first right, follow brown signs

The Gwaun valley has felt the hand of man for centuries. It is the source of the Stonehenge bluestones and indeed there is an iron age settlement in the grounds of the 600 year old farm dwelling that is Tregynon. With a rather more up-to-date take on dining out – but one still informed by tradition – the Heard family prepare and serve dinner party style meals to an appreciative clientele. Guests are asked to pre-order their main courses and an attentive ear is required when the menu is recited by telephone usually a day prior to arrival. Take aperitifs in a low ceilinged lounge with impressive inglenooks and prepare to enjoy simple, assured cooking like a starter of pan-fried chicken liver and home cured bacon salad or perhaps a pastry tartlet of walnut and brie. Main courses always feature a carefully prepared selection of fresh vegetables accompanying perhaps locally sourced rack of lamb or nicely aged sirloin steaks. Puddings have a homely feel but are all the more comforting for that. Chocolate fondant or 'the definitive' sticky toffee pudding are typical. The well chosen wine list has bins from a very reasonable £10.50.

Owners: Peter & Jane Heard  Chefs: Peter & Jane Heard, Gemma Cox
Open: Tues, Fri, Sat D only 7.30 – 8.00 (booking essential)
Closed: 2 weeks in winter/New Years Eve  Seats: 20  D £28.95

12/14  3 SC  P  V  r

Visa/Mastercard/Switch/Delta  Map reference 119

**Portmeirion, Gwynedd LL48 6EN**
**Tel: 01766 772400**
Email: castell@portmeirion-village.com
www.portmeirion-village.com
Off A487, signposted from Minffordd

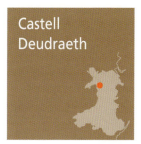

## Castell Deudraeth

The mock nineteenth-century castle stands in parkland on the edge of Portmeirion, an imposing grey-stone edifice that contrasts with the soft colours and contours of the Italianate village half a mile away. The restaurant, accessed from a large entrance hall filled with leather sofas, armchairs and low-slung coffee tables, occupies a light, relentlessly modern, dining room, with slate floor, floor to ceiling windows and blonde wood. À la carte lunches and dinners are served with help from blackboard specials, providing an uncommonly generous choice dealing in fashionable fare such as grilled sea bass with roasted fennel, spinach and aioli as well as crowd pleasers like lunchtime lamb burgers with spicy tomato salsa and chips, or local mussels in white wine and cream. Pen Llyn crab mayonnaise, Menai Straits oysters and plateau fruit de mer (with local lobster) are available seasonally and herb pancake filled with woodland mushrooms, leeks and Welsh goats' cheese is just one of a number of vegetarian dishes. Puddings vary from a rice pudding with poached summer fruits to chocolate truffle cake with ice cream. The wine list offers a good range with prices in keeping with the food.

Owner: Portmeirion Cyf  Chef: Steven Rowlands  Open: all week
L 12.00 – 2.00  D 6.00 – 9.30  Seats: 80  🍴  L £16.50  D £20.50

🛏11  🅿  ♿  Ⓥ  👶  🌿  ✖  🚭  🚻
Ⓒ Visa/Mastercard/Amex/Switch/Delta   Map reference

# Portmeirion

**Portmeirion, Gwynedd LL48 6ET**
**Tel: 01766 772440**
**Email: hotel@portmeirion-village.com**
**www.portmeirion-village.com**
Off A487, signposted from Minffordd

You can't fail to admire Sir Clough Williams-Ellis's magnificent Italianate folly on the Traeth Beach estuary, it is stunning whatever the weather with the village houses and cottages forming part of Portmeirion's highly individual hotel. Local produce is the foundation of Billy Taylor and David Doughty's bi-lingual menu. The food is an amalgamation of contemporary Welsh cooking and Mediterranean ideas, as in loin and cutlet of Welsh Lamb with sweet pumpkin mousseline, caramelised red onion tartlet, crispy pancetta and roasted garlic, for example, or fillet of Pen Llyn beef gratinated with Welsh rarebit on sourcroute, roasted shallots, turned potatoes and red wine jus. A fixed-price lunch menu offers three options per course (dinner twice that number) with salad of smoked chicken with fresh mozzarella, roasted plum tomatoes and balsamic dressing setting the ball rolling, followed by baked cod on mustard creamed leeks, mussels and dill butter sauce, with chocolate moelleux with crème anglaise and coconut tuille to finish. The wine list puts an emphasis on France, getting its teeth into most regions, yet keeps prices in check.

Owner: Portmeirion Cyf Chefs: Bill Taylor/David Doughty
Open: all week L 12.30 –2.00 D 7.00 – 9.00 Closed: 9th – 28th Jan
Seats: 100 L £14.50/16.50 D £22.50/37.50
30 40
Visa/Mastercard/Amex/Diners/Switch/Delta Map reference 121

**Nefyn Road, Pwllheli,
Gwynedd LL53 5TH
Tel: 01758 612363
Email: gunna@bodegroes.co.uk
www.bodegroes.co.uk**
On Nefyn Road (A497), one mile west of Pwllheli

Whichever way you look at it, this fine Georgian country house impresses both for its décor and for its professional service. The look is cool, minimal, tasteful, especially so in the dining room where modern lighting and wall-to-wall contemporary art are deployed with panache. Chris Chown's food moves with the times and seasons, uses local produce to good effect and offers a few luxuries that the surroundings demand, such as briefly seared foie gras and pigeon breast with an outstanding pigeon pastilla. A high degree of workmanship characterises much of the cooking, seen in a delicate mousseline of scallop, crab and laverbread with a well-judged crab sauce, and a stand-out rosemary kebab of mountain lamb with accompaniments of courgette provençale and garlic potatoes throwing the whole dish into sharp relief. Impressive desserts may include rich cardamom crème brûlée teamed with poached pears, while rhubarb and apple are sandwiched between cinnamon biscuits and served with elderflower custard. The wine list roams far and wide, taking in many fine producers, yet prices are remarkably restrained.

True Taste hospitality Gold 2002-3

Owners: Chris & Gunna Chown  Chef: Chris Chown  Open: L Sun 12.00 – 2.30  D Tues – Sat 7.00 – 9.30  Closed: Mid Dec-Jan  Seats: 40
L £17.50  D £38
16   11
C  Visa/Mastercard/Switch/Delta   Map reference

Ship Inn

**Red Wharf Bay, Anglesey LL75 8RJ**
**Tel: 01248 852568**
Take A5025, signposted Amlwch, approx 5 miles turn right, to Red Wharf Bay

Right on the shore at Traeth Coch and overlooking the sweep of the bay, the low white-washed Ship Inn occupies a row of 16th century fishermen's cottages. Quarry-tiled floors plus genuine exposed beams and stonework make for an interesting interior where the nautical memorabilia give the rambling bars great character. Arrive by boat at high tide, or early by car to bag a parking space as food is a big draw and the place really bustles on sunny days. The seasonal printed menu is supplemented by a changing chalkboard that lists locally landed fish and seafood and winter game dishes. Food is hearty, although there's a nod towards the Mediterranean with bouillabaisse and roast monkfish wrapped in Serrano ham with chorizo and basil mash and a red pepper coulis. Do expect dressed Ynys Mon crab, Conwy mussels with leeks, saffron and white wine, shank of local lamb with braised root vegetables and rosemary gravy and a tender, perfectly cooked Welsh rib-eye steak with Gorau Glas cheese and black pepper sauce. Puddings are well presented – try the excellent baked vanilla cheesecake with crunchy rhubarb compote. Imaginative lunchtime sandwiches, attentive young staff and well priced global wines complete the picture.

Owners: Andrew & Eve Kenneally Chef: Iwan Williams
Open: all week L 12.00 – 2.30 D 6.00 – 9.00 Closed: Christmas Day
Seats: 90 L £16 D £18
40
Visa/Mastercard/Switch/Delta  Map reference 123

**Redberth, Near Tenby,
Pembrokeshire SA70 8RP
Tel: 01646 651195**
On A477, Kilgetty to Pembroke,
East Williamson turn off

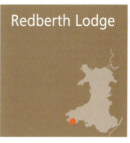

# Redberth Lodge

Set back off the main road Redberth Lodge is reached via a long drive. The newly completed bar overlooks the patio, which in summer is bursting with colourful baskets and tubs of flowers; perfect for enjoying a drink whilst selecting from the wide ranging menu. Light meals can be chosen from such offerings as home-made soup and pâté, savoury pancakes or tagliatelle with a choice of home-made sauces. For a more substantial meal, a starter of local goats' cheese grilled and served with a Pembrokeshire honey and balsamic dressing, might be followed by stir-fried prawns with chilli, ginger and courgettes, or Welsh Lamb pot roast with mint and cranberry, topped with herby dumplings, all served with good fresh vegetables. The vegetarian diner is certainly not forgotten here either and there is real imagination in herby coated polenta with roasted vegetables in a beetroot and paprika sauce and spinach tofu and red pepper curry are just two of the more imaginative options. Chef Chris Wooles and wife Anita create a relaxed, family atmosphere and their Sunday lunch is now a local institution making booking essential.

Owners: Chris & Anita Wooles Chef: Chris Wooles Open: Tues – Sun L 12.00 – 2.00 Tues – Sat D 6.00 – 9.00 Closed: Christmas Day/Boxing Day Seats: 70 L £13 D £22

90 SC P V

C Visa/Mastercard/Amex/Switch/Delta  Map reference

# Fairyhill

**Reynoldston, Gower, Swansea SA3 1BS**
**Tel: 01792 390139**
**Email: postbox@fairyhill.net**
**www.fairyhill.net**
Off A4118, 1.5 miles north-west of Reynoldston

Andrew Hetherington and Paul Davies have created a hotel that has justly attracted national acclaim for many years. Andrew leads a team of dedicated front of house staff who are warm, friendly and technically adept and Paul supervises one of the most celebrated kitchens in Wales. The charming house ticks all the country house hotel boxes – comfortable lounges, immaculate dining rooms and delightful bedrooms – but the whole is much more than that label would suggest. There is little stuffiness here and in many ways this is a country house hotel for the 21st century. The cuisine is informed, accurate and makes the very best use of the natural larder that is the Gower Peninsula. Salt marsh lamb is showcased in a dish of roast loin with pesto dressing and dumplings, Penclawdd cockles and laverbread may appear as frittata with bacon and spring onions (outstanding seafood is at the heart of many of the the deftly wrought dishes). The multi award winning wine list has been a labour of love for many years and bins are available which are almost impossible to find elsewhere. Oenophiles will appreciate the particularly impressive Bordeaux and Burgundy – both red and white – sections of the list.

Owners: Paul Davies & Andrew Hetherington  Chef: Bryony Jones
Open: all week L 12.30 – 2.00 D 7.30 – 9.00  Closed: First 2 weeks Jan
Seats: 60  L £18.95 D £37.50

Visa/Mastercard/Switch/Delta  Map reference 125

**Stonemill, Rockfield,
Near Monmouth NP25 5SW**
Tel: 01600 716273
www.thestonemill.co.uk
Located on the B4233, 2.5 miles from Monmouth town centre

This 16th century barn with its centrepiece stone cider mill has been converted into a modern stylish restaurant by owner Michelle DeCloedt – an engaging hostess and very much the friendly face of Stonemill. Enjoy an aperitif in the cosy bar before venturing down to the dining room which features exposed age-old timbers and an impressive vaulted ceiling. The restaurant is, however, right up-to-date in both cuisine and décor. The food is broadly Italian in style with quality ingredients to the fore and restrained cookery techniques which allow them to speak for themselves. Typical starters may include a punchy salad of marinated squid and anchovies or carefully sourced Italian meats served as antipasto. Roast suckling pig is something of a speciality and needs to be ordered in advance, or perhaps enjoy a classic Italian brodetto fish casserole with tomatoes and crisp chargrilled bruchetta. Puddings tend towards the simple – no bad thing that – with poached peaches served with pistachio nuts or home-made ice creams among the tempting options available. The wine list is concise and well sourced with a good selection of wines by the glass available.

Owners: Michelle DeCloedt Chef: Daniel Vaughn
Open: Tues – Sun L 12.00 – 2.00 Tues – Sat D 6.00 – 9.30
Closed: 2 weeks in January Seats: 56  L £10.50 D £25
12  6 SC P V
C Visa/Mastercard/Switch/Delta  Map reference

# Angel Inn

Salem

**Salem, Llandeilo, Carmarthenshire
SA19 7LY
Tel: 01558 823394**
Turn off the A40, towards Talley, then turn off left for Salem

The pristine Angel is still pub enough to have a comfy public bar, but its clusters of soft sofas and coffee tables hint that even a bite from the bar menu will be special. Step through to the dining area and the understated country style decor tips further towards restaurant, with subdued lighting, well spaced tables and smart, attentive staff clicking across bare wooden floorboards. Rod Peterson, a former Welsh Chef of the Year, cooks food that lives up to this sense of occasion: expect excellent ingredients, precisely cooked and presented with bags of technical ability and artistic flair (though Rod is aware enough of his setting to do this in slightly larger than life pub sized portions). The style is rooted in the classics but has plenty of modern twists. Starters could include a perfect soufflé of mature Welsh cheddar or an equally exact smoked haddock and spring onion tartlet, its buttery-light pastry and delicate flavour nicely rounded off with the tang of pineapple chutney and curry oil. Typical main courses include roast fillet of Welsh Beef with béarnaise sauce, puy lentils, spinach and bacon and roast rump of Welsh Lamb with an inspired, minty risotto of peas and feta cheese.

Owners: Rod Peterson & Elizabeth Smith  Chef: Rod Peterson
Open: Wed – Sat L 12.00 – 2.00 Tues – Sat D 7.00 – 9.00 Seats: 60
L £18 D £26

Visa/Mastercard/Switch/Delta   Map reference 127

**Sarnau, Near Cardigan,
Llanysul, Ceredigion SA44 6PE
Tel: 01239 810248
Email: welcome@penbontbren.com
www.penbontbren.com**
From Tan-y Groes, go north on A487, hotel is 2nd turning on right

Miles and Jacky Glossop are the kind of natural hosts who inspire a devoted following among their guests. Tucked away just a mile from the A487, Penbontbren consists of a farmhouse and its outbuildings, whose sympathetic conversion has included the creation of an on site farming museum. The restaurant occupies a spacious barn with exposed brick walls, pine furniture and a wood burning stove. The overall effect is neither trendy nor chintzy but comfortably traditional. The menu follows suit: Welsh classics such as bacon, cockles and laverbread or Welsh rarebit are shown at their very best. A keen awareness of flavours and the way they work together extends from saucing to vegetable accompaniments such as leeks cooked with mustard and cheese or spiced onions. Almost all the ingredients are local. Look out for the Rhydlewis terrine, using fish from a local smokery and sauces made with fruit from the garden – tender pieces of Welsh fillet steak, for example, could be marinated and served in a memorable sauce of cassis and juicy, home-grown blackcurrants. Finish with home-made desserts from the sweet trolley – perhaps a lemon meringue pie with a light-as-air topping.

Owners: Miles & Jacky Glossop Chefs: Miles & Jacky Glossop Open: D only all week 7.00 – 8.15 (booking essential) Closed: Christmas Day to 1st week in January Seats: 40 D £20
40 10 P r
C Visa/Mastercard/Amex/Switch/Delta   Map reference

## Saundersfoot

### St Brides

Saundersfoot,
Pembrokeshire SA69 9NH
Tel: 01834 812304
Email: reservations@stbrideshotel.com
www.stbrideshotel.com
Off the B4316 overlooking the sea

The impressive setting of St Brides Hotel with its spectacular views over the fishing village of Saundersfoot and Carmarthen Bay, provides a dramatic backdrop for diners eating in the appropriately named Cliff Restaurant. Don't let the view distract your attention from local boy Toby Goodwin's confident cookery though. Making good use of local Welsh produce Toby's menus feature intelligent use of such local delicacies as Carmarthen ham or Welsh salt marsh lamb. Just occasionally there can be a tendency to go a flavour too far in the composition of dishes, but when these impulses are reined in, as in a flavour-packed rump of lamb with thyme couscous and a red wine sauce, the kitchen is at its most assured. Puddings are a strong point – and who could resist a fresh take on autumnal flavours such as Bramley apple pannacotta with blackberry mille-feuille or a decadent sounding chocolate honeycomb parfait with oranges syrup? An extensive, well chosen wine list and eager to please staff help to complete the picture. Be sure to leave time to browse the carefully selected work on show by some of Wales's finest artists. Oh, and don't forget to book early and grab a window seat.

Owners: Andrew & Lindsay Evans Chef: Toby Goodwin Open: all week L 12.30 – 2.30 D 6.30 – 9.30 Seats: 100 L £18 D £28

50  37

C Visa/Mastercard/Amex/Switch/Delta  Map reference 129

**Skenfrith, Monmouthshire NP7 8UH**
**Tel: 01600 750235**
**Email: enquiries@skenfrith.co.uk**
**www.skenfrith.co.uk**
On the B4521, old Abergavenny to Ross-on-Wye road

This close to the border, The Bell could easily be a visitor's first encounter with eating out in Wales. If first impressions count then this place is doing the nation proud as a standard bearer. The 17th century building with its whitewashed exterior is an enticement in itself, set in a beautiful valley by a stone bridge over the Monnow. It's a setting of crisp, rural simplicity and seems totally in tune with its surroundings from the uncomplicated but stylish interior, through the friendly but unfussy service, to food that doesn't fall into the trap of over-complication. There is a real respect for ingredients apparent in dishes like rump of Monmouthshire lamb with blue cheese mash and red wine sauce where the lamb arrives perfectly pink and with a delicate flavour to match. The lunch menu offers a slightly simplified version of the menu with open pita bread sandwiches amongst the options, but even the simplest salads (rocket and feta or bresaola with avocado salsa) are handled with unusual sensitivity. The wine list is an extraordinary triumph of enthusiasm and with so many good vintages you may be tempted to really splash out.

True Taste hospitality Silver 2003-4

**Owners:** Jane & William Hutchings **Chef:** Kurt Fleming **Open:** all week April – Oct, Tues – Sun Nov – March L 12.00 – 2.30 D 7.00 – 9.00 **Closed:** 23rd Jan – 10th Feb **Seats:** 80 L £23.87 D £25.51

40   8   P   V   r

C  Visa/Mastercard/Amex/Switch   Map reference

## Solva — Old Pharmacy

5 Main Street, Solva,
Near Haverfordwest SA62 6UU
Tel: 01437 720005
Email: theoldpharmacy@btinternet.com
www.theoldpharmacy.co.uk
In the heart of lower Solva fishing village

Here's a breath of fresh air: 'Choose anything in any order and quantity,' urges the menu at The Old Pharmacy. If you only want a starter, or perhaps an espresso and a home-made dessert, that's fine. The interior reflects this relaxed attitude, with cheerful colours, modern artwork, warm lighting and a diplomatic mix of background music. Owner Martin Lawton heads an efficient, friendly team of staff who allow you to take the meal at your own pace. The menu bounds enthusiastically through local ingredients and global spices, offering up some very effective combinations – a fresh sea bass, for instance, stuffed with ginger, spring onion and sea salt then coated in spicy breadcrumbs and deep fried, which simply sings with flavour. Precisely cooked seasonal veg round it off nicely. Even when the flavours don't go zing, as with a starter of fish soup, the dish is still competently handled, the flavours balanced and enjoyable. The stream at the bottom of the pretty cottage garden runs down to Solva harbour, the source, along with the port of Milford Haven, of a steady supply of fresh fish and shellfish. Meat options could include organic Welsh Black beef, while vegetarian options such as a crumble of devilled mushrooms, are clearly more than an afterthought.

Owner: Martin Lawton Chefs: Matthew Ricketts & Tom Phillips Open: all week D only 5.30 – 9.30 Closed: Christmas Eve/Christmas Day/Boxing Day & 3rd Jan – 10th Feb Seats: 70 D £26

50

Visa/Mastercard/Switch/Delta Map reference 131

52 Beach Road, Southerndown,
Bridgend CF32 0RP
Tel: 01656 880127
Email: dougwindsor34@aol.com
From M4, head towards Bridgend,
Ogmore by Sea

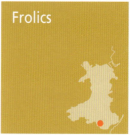

# Frolics

## Southerndown

If it were not for the salty breezes blowing in off the Bristol Channel the unassuming redbrick building that houses Frolics might give you the impression of a neighbourhood restaurant in a city suburb somewhere. It would be a fortunate neighbourhood. Frolics is a diminutive operation with just a handful of tables, a small bar and the kitchen just beyond. It's compact enough that you can hear the occasional clatter from the kitchen where Doug Windsor and his team produce Francophile cooking that is sometimes intricate but always well-balanced and intelligently conceived. A good value lunch menu offers the most direct dishes such as a chicken liver and wild mushroom terrine with onion marmalade or a fillet of Usk salmon with a rocket and parmesan salad and sun-blushed tomato dressing. The à la carte offers a little more complexity but the combinations – say Pembroke crab and sweet chilli risotto wrapped in wilted leaves or rump of Welsh mountain lamb with fondant potato and tarragon jus, are sensibly rooted in the classic. The wine list shows care in selection, there's some real character from France and mark-ups are restrained.

Owner: Doug Windsor Chef: Doug Windsor Open: L Tues – Sun 12.00 – 2.00 D Tues – Sat 6.00 – 10.00 Closed: Boxing Day Seats: 50 L £11.95 D £28.95

30

C Visa/Mastercard/Amex/Diners/Switch/Delta  Map reference 132

## Inn at the Elm Tree

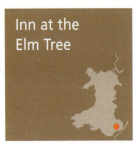

St Brides, Wentlooge,
Newport NP10 8SQ
Tel: 01633 680225
Email: inn@the-elm-tree.co.uk
www.the-elm-tree.co.uk
M4, junction 28, coast road for 4 miles

The traditional and the thoroughly up-to-date sit very comfortably together at this charming inn located a mere ten minutes off the M4 motorway. The restaurant with its stripped down black and white minimalism contrasts with and complements the flagstone floored original inn. The bedrooms available are all individually styled to very high standards. The food offering is straightforward in approach with hearty portions of well prepared food being the order of the day. Typical dishes could include tempura of sole with a lemon dressing or a delightfully simple dressed crab main course with crisp crostini. Some real ambition is evident in constructions such as venison loin with herb mash and a black cherry and port sauce but this kitchen gives of its best when things are kept simple. Traditional puddings like lemon posset and Eton mess are both satisfying and comforting. Staff clearly enjoy looking after their guests here and offer attentive and engaging service. The wine list features about 50 bins of familiar favourites with a few high end stunners such as Chateau Lafite or an exceptional Puligny Montrachet available to diners for whom expense is not an issue.

Owners: Mrs Thomas & Mr Ellis  Chef: Shaun Ellis  Open: all week
L 12.00 – 2.30  D 6.00 – 10.00  Seats: 65  L £10  D £25
25  13
C  Visa/Mastercard/Amex/Switch/Delta  Map reference 133

**16 Nun Street, St Davids,
Pembrokeshire SA62 6NS
Tel: 01437 729220
Email: lawtonsatno16@aol.com**
25 yards off the Cross Square

An air of simple, effortless style is created here with crisp white walls, bright original artwork, wooden floors and pale, modern furniture. Just below the buzz of conversation drifts that easy, Nora Jones brand of background music that might have been designed with places like this in mind. From the comprehensive wine list to the heavenly home-made fudge with coffee, the experience is thoughtfully put together with plenty of personal touches. A team of young, friendly staff deliver efficient service while chef Stephen Lawton occasionally emerges from the kitchen to meet his diners. Stephen's food – modern, unpretentious and beautifully presented – is underpinned by quality ingredients, including local delicacies such as Ramsey Sound lobster. Begin with the likes of fresh crab and gruyere tart or cream of pea and celery soup, its delicate flavour enhanced by melting chunks of dolcelatte. Main courses could include succulent free-range chicken breast roasted with herbs and white wine and served with a light leek and mushroom cream sauce or fillet of Welsh organic beef on a horseradish suet pudding with red wine sauce. Be sure to leave room for home-made desserts such as baked Alaska made with home-made coconut ice cream then garnished with exotic fruit and decadent chocolate sauce.

Owners: Stephen & Kim Lawton   Chef: Stephen Lawton
Open: Tues – Sun D only 6.00 – 9/9.30   Closed: Christmas Day/
Boxing Day/New Years Day   Seats: 38   🍽   £28

**P** **V** 👤 🍁 ✕ 🍴

**C** Visa/Mastercard/Switch/Delta   Map reference 134

# Morgan's Brasserie

**20 Nun Street, St Davids, Pembrokeshire SA62 6NT**
Tel: 01437 720508
Email: morgans@stdavids.co.uk
www.morgans-in-stdavids.co.uk
60 yards from Cross Square in town centre, past the Cathedral Close entrance

A change of regime since the last edition of the guide (Ceri Morgan can now be found at Ramsey House – see entry) but this diminutive St Davids restaurant seems to remain as popular as ever. Physically, little has changed and the trad bistro feel is still there right down to the specials blackboard that supplements the regular menu. Wisely, it's the fish dishes that make up most of the former selection allowing the kitchen the flexibility to source according to the best available. There's not too much mucking about with the raw materials here and dishes like sea bass served on a bed of roasted vegetables are notable for the careful cooking of the fish and the accuracy of seasoning to bring out the full flavour. Portions are generous – a starter of black pudding and Stilton salad would probably do as a main-course for some – and there are enough meat options (featuring the likes of Welsh salt marsh lamb) to please the carnivores. Staff are eager to please and manage to keep service well-paced even when things are at their busiest. The wine list offers plenty of choice from around the globe and prices are mostly in the pocket-friendly bracket.

Owners: Richard Drakeley, Linda Hurley and Lynsey Draycott
Chef: Richard Drakeley Open: all week (may vary in low season)
L 12.30 – 2.30 D 7.00 – 10.00 Seats: 36 L £15 D £30
12/36
Visa/Mastercard/Switch/Delta Map reference 135

**Lower Moor, St Davids,
Pembrokeshire SA62 6RP
Tel: 01437 720321
info@ramseyhouse.co.uk
www.ramseyhouse.co.uk**
At Cross Square take Goats Street towards Port Clais

After more than 10 years running their eponymous restaurant in the centre of St Davids, Ceri and Elaine Morgan have moved to Ramsey House – a cosy, modern guest house on the edge of the town. It looks a world away from their old restaurant but Ceri's cooking and Elaine's front of house skills have survived intact, making this a particularly good choice for anyone who wants a good value combination of accommodation and quality food. The whole operation has been scaled down a lot since their Morgan's days – just five or six small tables and a modest but tempting choice of food and wine. Starters could include Ceri Morgan's own inventions such as gravad lax made with home-cured sewin or double duck terrine – a rustic combination of duck liver pâté with shredded duck confit. Main courses such as lemon sole stuffed with prawns and served with a white wine cream sauce come with wonderful crispy roast potatoes and an interesting mix of vegetables. But the star of the show is the desserts – perhaps a crisp and soft hazelnut pavlova with forest fruits or Ceri's ever popular home-made ice creams.

Owners: Ceri & Elaine Morgan  Chef: Ceri Morgan
Open: Thurs – Sat D only 7.00 – 8.00 (may vary)
Closed: Christmas Day  Seats: 18  D £24

18  7  P
No Credit Cards  Map reference  136

## Warpool Court

**St Davids, Pembrokeshire SA62 6BN**
**Tel: 01437 720300**

From the centre of St Davids, bear left from Cross Square, following signs

The brochure for this mansion house hotel sets out its stall with enthusiastic quotations from visiting Lords and Ladies, so expect classic, country house elegance – a place to relax in a deep sofa with a copy of Country Living or stroll in the gardens after a game of croquet. The surroundings add to the air of hushed tranquillity: mature, well tended grounds give way to a broad sweep of green that runs down towards St Non's well, an ancient healing spring still used today. Beyond that – on almost all sides – is the sea. The dining room, smartly and simply decorated in pink and cream, is filled with that soft, bright light that comes with sea views. Underpinned by classic French techniques but full of modern touches, the menu opens with the likes of quail and Carmarthen ham sausage with fried potatoes, puy lentils and thyme jus or a meaty, herby duck rillet with red onion marmalade and toasted brioche. Typical main courses include best end of lamb with fondant potato, aubergine purée, roast red pepper and courgette and rosemary jus or roast pork fillet with cabbage and bacon, parmentier potatoes, caramelised apple and cider sauce. In short, expect high quality ingredients, cooked with flair and beautifully presented. The wine list is good too.

Owner: Peter Trier Chef: John Daniels Open: all week L 12.00 – 1.45
D 7.00 – 9.15 Closed: January Seats: 60 L £29 D £49
22  25
Visa/Mastercard/Amex/Diners/Switch/Delta  Map reference  137

**17 St Mary Street, Swansea SA1 3LH**
Tel: 01792 464068
www.thechelseacafe.co.uk
Just off Wind Street

# Chelsea Restaurant

Swansea

The Rennie-Mackintosh inspired frontage of this intimate side street restaurant contrasts with a design conscious contemporary interior. Stripped wood floors and bleached, blonde wood tongue and groove walls hung with abstract paintings (which are available for purchase) in the style of Piet Mondrian, set the scene. Mat Hole's informed, ingredient driven cuisine has a strong seafood bias and his intelligent use of local delicacies such as Penclawdd laverbread and cockles speaks of a chef who knows howto source and utilise fine produce. Menus at the Chelsea Café are intelligently written and the dishes avoid the pitfalls of over complication and excessive garnishing. Typical of the style could be a light, well flavoured French fish soup (more like a bisque than a bouillabaisse) with sea bass, salmon and prawns which comes as a hearty main course. A fairly short dessert selection tends towards the classical and guests can expect to enjoy competently handled dishes like a pot au chocolate with vanilla ice cream. A handful of wines are available by the glass whilst those pushing the boat out may like to snap up the likes of Cloudy Bay Sauvignon Blanc for under £30.

Owner: Mat Hole Chef: Mat Hole Open: Tues – Sat L 12.00 – 2.30 D 7.00 – 9.30 Closed: Bank Holidays/Christmas Seats: 55
🍽 L £12.95 D £25
👥 40 [V] ♿ ✿ ✕ 🚬
[C] Visa/Mastercard/Switch/Delta  Map reference 138

# Didier & Stephanie

**56 St Helen's Road, Swansea SA1 4BE**
**Tel: 01792 655603**
**Email: Stedanvel@hotmail.com**
In city centre

If you fancy a little piece of France without leaving Wales, then you'd have to work hard to find a better candidate than this small Swansea restaurant. Its diminutive scale means that the two principles (Didier's at the stove whilst Stephanie handles front of house) manage much of the operation themselves and they bring a bright informality to both the food and the service that stirs memories of meals taken in rural France. Menus offer plenty of choice without being unmanageably long and the English descriptions are followed by evocative French translations. Dishes are classic and all the better for that. A lunchtime menu might offer a faithful pork terrine followed by casseroled rabbit with a mustard sauce, finishing with a light and delicious almond and cherry cake served with an almond ice cream. It's worth noting that lunch is excellent value although dinner prices are far from exorbitant either. The dining room is intimate with simple country furnishings that fit in well with the style of the food and the cheerful, easygoing service. The wine list is relatively brief but should meet most tastes, although the lack of information on growers and estates doesn't aid selection.

Owners: Didier Suvé & Stephanie Danvel Chef: Didier Suvé
Open: Tues – Sat L 12.00 – 1.30 D 7.00 – 8.30/9.00 Seats: 28
L £12.70 D £22

Visa/Mastercard/Switch/Delta Map reference 139

# Grand

Swansea

Ivey Place, High Street,
Swansea SA1 1NX
Tel: 01792 645898
Opposite Swansea railway station

This grand old railway hotel has recently been given a new lease of life, completely refurbished and stylishly reinvented for the new millennium. The design conscious interior is smart and contemporary with the Beaches Restaurant featuring modish chocolate leather seating, stripped wood floors and – perhaps incongruously – a plasma screen showing Sky TV. The kitchen is open to view and the busy chefs are a rather more engaging form of entertainment. The cooking is certainly designed to impress, with extra courses such as amuse-bouche, pre-desserts and even a pre-main course adding to the traditional three-course structure. Expect carefully handled dishes such as roast suckling pig with crisp crackling, pan fried apple and a grain mustard sauce or Thai style chicken breast with zesty lemongrass, sautéed leaves and a coconut and red chilli broth. Simple puddings may include Champagne sorbet, vanilla pod ice cream or a more technically impressive summer berry terrine. Service was suffering from a few teething problems on a visit soon after opening but was invariably helpful and polite. The wine list is well chosen and features a nice selection available by the glass.

**S**

Owner: Con Maloney Open: L all week 12.00 – 2.30 D Tues – Sat 6.30 – 10.00 Seats: 52 L £15 D £25

32

C Visa/Mastercard/Amex/Switch  Map reference

# Hurrens Inn on the Estuary

**13 Station Road, Loughor,
Swansea SA4 6TR
Tel: 01792 899092
Email: hurrens@hotmail.com**

M4 Junction 47, follow A484 to Llanelli, (do not cross Loughor bridge) and take first left into Station Road

Perched on the site of a Roman fort, Hurrens has a picturesque and historical location. There's nothing backward looking about the restaurant, though, which is modern in both decoration and outlook. The menu, which makes extensive use of local Welsh ingredients, is Mediterranean-influenced with passing touches of the orient. Seafood is a strength here, you might for instance start with pan-fried tiger prawns and sweet chilli dipping sauce and follow up with the roast monkfish wrapped in Parma ham. Mahi mahi and locally caught sea bass also make an appearance. Other local specialities include glazed shank of Gower lamb with fondant potatoes or chargrilled sirloin of Welsh Beef with béarnaise sauce. Friendly, relaxed and attentive staff will try to help as you agonise over the list of home-made desserts which might include caramelised bananas, toffee sauce and clotted cream or whisky bread and butter pudding. A well balanced, international wine list complements the exact cooking. Don't miss a chance to check out the good value lunchtime and Sunday lunch menus.

Owners: Graham & Mary Hurren  Chef: Graham Hurren
Open: Wed – Sun L 12.00 – 2.30 Mon – Sat D 6.30 – 9.30
Closed: Christmas Day  Seats: 32  L £11  D £21.50

Visa/Mastercard/Amex/Diners/Switch/Delta  Map reference **141**

**Somerset Place, Swansea SA1 1RR**
**Tel: 01792 484848**
Email: fdesk@morganshotel.co.uk
www.morganshotel.co.uk
Located in the Marina quarter, in city centre, adjacent to Wind Street and Swansea Museum

Martin and Louisa Morgan's stylish hotel has quickly grown to be a thriving centre of Swansea social life. Period architectural features combine with elegant contemporary décor to create an ambience unique in the city. Morgan's Restaurant occupies the space that once was the boardroom of the Port Authority and the hardwood parquet flooring, ornate plasterwork and antique chandeliers reflect Swansea's significant role in maritime history. Now revitalised as a thoroughly 21st century brasserie; chef Chris Keenan has a strong local following for his take on modern cuisine. Expect such dishes as duck spring roll with plum sauce and wok fried noodles or the popular comfort dish braised rabbit with a creamy cider and Dijon mustard sauce. Chris is keen to make good use of local ingredients and Welsh Black beef and salt marsh lamb regularly feature. Puddings could include a rich chocolate pot, perhaps with prune and Armagnac ice cream and there is a good selection of well kept cheeses available. Staff are enthusiastic but there can be some hiccups on occasion. The extensive, well chosen wine list runs to 150 bins with 10 house wines providing good value for money.

Owners: Martin & Louisa Morgan  Chef: Chris Keenan
Open: all week L 12.00 – 3.00 D 6.30 – 10.15  Seats: 120
L £15 D £30

24  20

Visa/Mastercard/Amex/Switch/Delta  Map reference

# Windsor Lodge

**Mount Pleasant, Swansea SA1 6EG**
**Tel: 01792 642158**
**Email: reservations@windsor-lodge.co.uk**
**www.windsor-lodge.co.uk**
Bottom of Mount Pleasant hill, on left, just past police station

Chef Tina Stewart's confident cooking continues to be a considerable asset to the stylish Windsor Lodge. Owners Ron and Pam Rumble have run the hotel for over 30 years but there are no signs of staleness. Guests are invited to have a drink in the cosy bars and lounges before being escorted through to the elegant dining room. Tina's cuisine is straightforward and to the point with little pretence but bags of flavour. Home-made crusty bread rolls are a real treat and speak of the dedication at work in this kitchen. Tina is not afraid to include some real comfort dish classics in her repertoire so look out for the occasional pie; beefsteak and ale, if you are lucky. Highlights, typical of the style here, include a delicious Oriental crispy duck salad with a plum dressing, crunchy bean sprouts, baby spinach and watercress. Crispy skinned and deliciously fresh sea bass may come roasted with Puy lentils, leeks, bacon and a punchy grain mustard dressing. Be sure to leave room for one of the confidently handled puddings; treats such as zesty lemon and orange tart require willpower to refuse. The sensibly concise wine list offers plenty of keenly priced bottles for under £15.

Owners: Ron & Pam Rumble Chef: Tina Stewart Open: L by arrangement D Mon – Sat 7.30 – 9.00 Closed: Dec 22nd – Jan 2nd Seats: 20 L £18 D £24

32  19

Visa/Mastercard/Amex/Diners/Switch/Delta  Map reference 143

**79 – 81 Talbot Road,
Talbot Green, Llantrisant,
Rhondda Cynon Taf CF72 8AE
Tel: 01443 239600
Email: staffbrookes@btconnect.com
www.brookes-restaurant.co.uk**
Junction 34, M4, onto dual carriageway, towards Llantrisant, turn left for Talbot Green

Appearances can certainly be deceptive. On the outside, two terraced houses brightly painted; inside, a white walled mirrored labyrinth of cool minimalist chic. When presented with the menu, however, all such complications cease. What you see is definitely what you get. Delicious light twice baked goats' cheese soufflé on a bed of toasted pine kernels, rocket and sun-blushed tomatoes is brimming with flavour, while smoked salmon with a sauté of new potatoes, spring onions and crab meat is another good choice to start. The mix of Oriental and Mediterranean concepts and ingredients continues with mains such as pan-fried cod with a curried seafood velouté and crispy seaweed or seared fillet of sea bass on a stir-fry of tiger prawns, aromatic greens, and soy reduction. Brasserie favourites such as Welsh sirloin steak with peppercorn or mustard sauce also sit easy on the menu. The good quality house wines complement the meal well. Desserts might include the classic Eton Mess: a combination of strawberries, meringue and whipped cream served with lemon curd ice cream, or raspberry and white chocolate crème brulée.

Owners: Kevin & Craig Brookes  Chef: Craig Brookes
Open: L Tues – Fri & Sun 12.00 – 2.30 D Tues – Sat (Plus Mon in Dec) 7 – 10 Closed: Christmas Eve/Boxing Day/1st & 2nd Jan Seats:91
L £14.95 D £28  26

Visa/Mastercard/Amex/Diners/Switch/Delta  Map reference 144

# Mews Bistro

**Upper Frog Street, Tenby,
Pembrokeshire SA70 7JD
Tel: 01834 844068
www.mewsbistrotenby.co.uk**
Within the town walls, at the end of the Mews Walkway

Ask anyone locally where the best restaurants are to be found in Tenby and the chances are that the Mews will feature in their answer. Situated in a tucked away location (at the end of a mews naturally) in the heart of the town, the L shaped dining room is invariably bustling by early evening. There is a cheerful, easygoing feeling to the whole operation with staff that cope admirably with the sudden onrush of hungry customers. The food is appropriately no-nonsense but it would be a mistake not to recognise that there is clearly someone in the kitchen who cares about the quality of the produce and knows how to pack plenty of flavour into a dish. The menu is fairly extensive once you take the daily specials into account and rightly given the location, features a good deal of fish as well as good steaks. The former might feature main-courses such as a thick fillet of sea bass served simply with lemon and herb butter or pan-fried gurnard with sweet potato mash and marjoram butter. Oak smoked salmon served warm in a filo tart with fennel is also typical of the robust full-flavoured style. Quantities are as generous as the flavours. A wine list of about 30 bins offers a good range and prices rarely creep above £15.

Owners: Mike Evans & Andrew Swales  Chef: Andrew Swales
Open: D only Mon – Sat (Apr – Oct) Wed – Sat (Nov – Mar)
6.30 – 9.30  Closed: Christmas Day/Boxing Day  Seats: 85  D £22

Visa/Mastercard/Switch/Delta  Map reference 145

**Lon Isallt, Trearddur Bay,
Anglesey LL65 2UW
Tel: 01407 860006**
Exit A55 for Valley, in Valley turn left for Trearddur Bay, next to RNLI

Waterfront

Trearddur Bay

Smack beside the beautiful curving beach and looking out across the wide bay this modern, slate-roofed building enjoys a superb setting. Expect a minimalist interior with lofty ceilings, café-style tables and chairs and big windows. The atmosphere is relaxed and informal and its location means it attracts a wide and varied clientele. With a sun-trap terrace accessible from the beach, it's more café-bar than restaurant at lunchtime, with sunbathers and families retreating in search of sandwiches and light meals. The latter take in pasta meals, favourites like ham, egg and chips and home-made beefburgers and simple seafood dishes in the form of steamed mussels marinière and a delicious fresh fillet of natural smoked haddock topped with Y Fenni cheese. Cooking moves up a gear in the evenings. The more innovative, seasonally changing menu offers locally caught fish and seafood – turbot with potatoes, spinach and red wine, sea bass with sauce vierge – and quality meats from local suppliers. Typically, choose rump of lamb with red bean purée and cumin-roasted carrots, or braised belly pork with a pear and herb crust. Precede with a terrine of chicken, ham and mushrooms and finish with lemon tart or a plate of British cheeses.

Owners: W Roberts, S Dale, T Carpenter Chefs: M Hodgkinson & W Roberts & Open: all week (closed Mon & Tues out of season) L 12.00 – 2.30 D 6.00 – 9.30 (7.00 – 9.00 in winter) Closed: Boxing Day/New Years Day Seats: 90 L £14 D £23 30 Visa/Mastercard/Amex/Switch/Delta Map reference 146

# Tredunnock

## Newbridge

Tredunnock, Near Usk,
Monmouthshire NP15 1LY
Tel: 01633 451000
Email: thenewbridge@tinyonline.co.uk
www.thenewbridge.co.uk
From Usk, take B route to Llangibby,
1 mile past Llangibby see sign for
Hotel/Restaurant

Tucked away between Usk and Caerleon, The Newbridge isn't the easiest place to find on your first visit. It's well worth the effort though and you may well find that once you've located it, you're amongst the many loyal customers who regularly beat a path to the door. If you should chance upon an idyllic summers day, the advice is to take a seat out on the terrace. The seating options are many though, as this is a building with several levels all furnished in contemporary fashion and offering the opportunity to sample some really good modern cooking. The seasonally changing main body of the menu has a welcome emphasis on local produce such as Monmouthshire lamb, Welsh Beef and Bwlch venison, and these are supplemented by a specials menu that offers a wide selection of fish. The latter might include a starter of delicately handled marinated crayfish with a spaghetti of vegetables or main-courses that might centre on sea bass, cod and monkfish. Desserts show real imagination, as in a small trio of delicious honey roasted pears with pistachio semi-freddo. A comprehensive wine list has a long list of Champagnes and is particularly strong on new world bins.

Owner: Glen Rick Court Ltd Chef: Iain Sampson Open: all week
L 12.00 – 2.30 (4.00 on Sun) D 6.30 (Sun 7.00) – 9.30 (Sun 8.30)
Closed: Boxing Day/New Years Day Seats: 80 L £12.50 D £26
16/80 6
C Visa/Mastercard/Amex/Diners/Switch/Delta Map reference 147

**Walterstone, Herefordshire HR2 0DU**
**Tel: 01873 890307**
**Email: reception@allthotel.co.uk**
**www.allthotel.co.uk**

Allt-yr-Ynys

Walterstone

This imposing country house property straddles the border with England and serves as a good first impression for anyone about to venture deeper into the country. The classically styled dining room is attractively proportioned and the sense of calm is only occasionally interrupted by background music. Start with a carefully crafted dish of crisply battered haddock strips with rocket salad, crunchy straw potatoes and tangy hollandaise sauce or sample a classic warm salad; perhaps chicken livers with cherry tomatoes, bacon, French beans and dressed salad leaves. Main courses showcase deft fingers at work in the kitchen with the likes of boned out braised shank of lamb being accompanied by the curiously labelled 'confit' of leeks, roast potatoes, crisp garlic and red wine jus. Fish may appear as pan-fried skate wing with chive scented crushed potatoes, braised asparagus and a piquant caper and parsley dressing. Puddings show a sense of adventure in their flavour combinations – expect such assemblies as wine poached pear with orange and cardamom scented pannacotta and strawberry water ice or banana fritters with chocolate ice cream and a blackcurrant compote.

W

Owners: Howard & Elaine Williams  Chef: Ian Jackson
Open: Tues – Sun L 12.00 – 2.00 all week D 7.00 – 9.30
Seats: 40  L £20 D £30
100  21
C Visa/Mastercard/Amex/Switch/Delta  Map reference 148

# Stone Hall

**Welsh Hook, Haverfordwest, Pembrokeshire SA62 5NS**
**Tel: 01348 840212**
**www.stonehall-mansion.co.uk**
Just off A40 north of Haverfordwest

Since 1984 French born Martine Watson has been running this beautiful manor house in the style of a French auberge. Accessed via a short winding drive, the house, set in ten acres, is surrounded by rhododendrons and azaleas, making a spring visit a must. Not surprisingly the menu has its roots in France, with snails in garlic butter, marmite du pecheur (aromatic fish broth) and salad of duck confit making an appearance. Cooking is accomplished and skilful use is made of top quality local produce such as beef, lamb, venison and fish. Superb local turbot is served in a langoustine sauce and loin of venison is flash roasted and served with spiced pear and a rich game sauce. Puddings are uncomplicated but good; profiteroles are filled with ice cream and served with melted chocolate, succulent baked peaches filled with amaretti and nougat glacé with red fruits. Flag-stoned floors and oak beams feature throughout and Martine's love of cats creates a theme with cat related trinkets and pictures popping up everywhere. The restaurant has a cottagey feel and boasts a slate floor, stone walls and an impressive inglenook fireplace.

Owner: Martine Watson Chef: Marion Evans Open: Tues – Sat D only 7.00 – 9.30 Closed: Christmas Day/Boxing Day/1 week in Nov, 2 weeks in Jan/Feb Seats: 30 D £30

15  4

Visa/Mastercard/Amex/Diners/Switch/Delta  Map reference 149

**Whitebrook, Near Monmouth, Monmouthshire NP25 4TX**
Tel: 01600 860254
Email: crown@whitebrook.demon.co.uk
www.crownatwhitebrook.co.uk
North of Chepstow on A466 left turn for Whitebrook

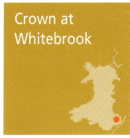

# Crown at Whitebrook

The narrow winding road that eventually leads to The Crown is a well-worn one as far as lovers of good food are concerned. Perched amongst the trees on the side of a valley, there is a gentle peace about the place that makes it an ideal setting to give proper attention to the excellent food and contemplate a wine list compiled with real enthusiasm. There is also something very French about the place, most obviously in the cooking which is rooted in the classic but also shows a depth of flavour and a dexterity reminiscent of meals taken across the channel. Menu descriptions tend to give you all the details, so dishes can sound complex but happily when they arrive they are conceived with an intelligence and unity. Simple pork rillettes come with a fruity chutney and are typically well-seasoned with similar virtues apparent in a main course of sea bass served with a crunchy, herbed couscous. There is obvious attention paid to the sourcing of top-notch produce whether it be a superb canon of lamb or a perfect rhubarb tart with flawless pastry. Couple all this with service that is attentive and appropriately relaxed and you can see why so many make the pilgrimage.

Owners: Jonathan & Nicola Davies  Chef: James Sommerin
Open: Tues – Sun L 12.00 – 2.00  Tues – Sat D 7.00 – 9.00
Closed: Dec 17th – Jan 17th  Seats: 32  L £19 D £30

12  10  P  V  

C  Visa/Mastercard/Switch  Map reference  150

# Index A – L

## With map and page numbers

698 **99**, p128

## A

| | |
|---|---|
| Allt Yr Ynys | **148**, p177 |
| Amser Da | **86**, p115 |
| Angel, Abergavenny | **5**, p34 |
| Angel Inn, Llandellio | **73**, p102 |
| Angel Inn, Salem | **127**, p156 |
| Armless Dragon | **30**, p59 |

## B

| | |
|---|---|
| Bae Abermaw | **14**, p43 |
| Barn at Brynich | **21**, p50 |
| Bear | **51**, p80 |
| Bell | **130**, p159 |
| Black Bear | **18**, p47 |
| Boat | **57**, p86 |
| Bobs | **98**, p127 |
| Bodidris Hall | **72**, p101 |
| Bodysgallen Hall | **77**, p106 |
| Brasserie, Beaumaris | **16**, p45 |
| Brasserie, Hawarden | **61**, p90 |
| Brookes | **144**, p173 |
| Bryn Tyrch | **29**, p58 |
| Bully's | **31**, p60 |
| Butchers Arms | **70**, p99 |

## C

| | |
|---|---|
| Café Niçoise | **47**, p76 |
| Carlton House | **91**, p120 |
| Castell Deudraeth | **120**, p149 |
| Castle Cottage | **58**, p87 |
| Castle | **48**, p77 |
| Chandlery | **107**, p136 |
| Chelsea Restaurant | **138**, p167 |
| Claudes | **100**, p129 |
| Clytha Arms | **6**, p35 |
| Cnapan | **110**, p139 |

# Index

Coed-y-Mwstwr **24**, p53
Conrah **11**, p40
Corner House **114**, p143
Cornmill **82**, p111
Cors **65**, p94
Court Colman **25**, p54
Crown at Whitebrook **150**, p179

## D

Da Castaldo **32**, p61
Da Venditto **33**, p62
Didier & Stephanie **139**, p168
Drovers Rest **92**, p121
Druidstone **27**, p56
Dulais Rock **3**, p32
Dylanwad Da **56**, p85

## E

Egerton Grey **15**, p44

## F

Fairyhill **125**, p154
Falcon **43**, p72
Farmers Arms **54**, p83
Felin Fach Griffin **22**, p51
Foxhunter **106**, p135
Fredericks **101**, p130
Frolics **132**, p161

## G

George's **60**, p89
Gilby's **34**, p63
Glasfryn **97**, p126
Grand **140**, p169
Granvilles **50**, p79
Great House **26**, p55

## H

Harbourmaster **1**, p30
Harp Inn **111**, p140
Harry's **12**, p41
Holland House **35**, p64
Huddarts **49**, p78
Hurrens **141**, p170
Hurst House **66**, p95

## I

Inn at the Elm Tree **133**, p162
Izakaya **36**, p65

## J

Junction 28 **108**, p137

## K

Kinmel Arms **9**, p38
Knights **102**, p131

## L

La Marina & El Puerto **37**, p66
Lake Country House **81**, p110
Lake Vyrnwy **90**, p119
Lasswade **93**, p122
Lawtons at No 16 **134**, p163
Le Gallois **116**, p145
Le Gallois – Y Cymro **38**, p67
Leadon's Brasserie **75**, p104
Llangoed Hall **94**, p123
Llansantffraed Court **89**, p118
Llanwenarth **7**, p36
Lobster Pot **46**, p75

# Index M – Y

## With map and page numbers

Le Gallois Y Cymro

### M
| | | |
|---|---|---|
| Maes-y-Neuadd | **59**, p88 |
| Mermaid | **103**, p132 |
| Mews Bistro | **145**, p174 |
| Milebrook House | **64**, p93 |
| Morgans | **142**, p171 |
| Morgan's Brasserie | **135**, p164 |

### N
| | |
|---|---|
| Nant Ddu Lodge | **53**, p82 |
| Nantyffin Cider Mill | **52**, p81 |
| Newbridge | **147**, p176 |
| Norton House | **104**, p133 |

### O
| | |
|---|---|
| Old Black Lion | **62**, p91 |
| Old Kings Arms | **113**, p142 |
| Old Pharmacy | **131**, p160 |
| Old Point House | **13**, p42 |
| Old Post Office | **39**, p68 |
| Old Rectory | **87**, p116 |
| Olive Tree | **115**, p144 |
| Owens | **109**, p138 |

### P
| | |
|---|---|
| Palé Hall | **71**, p100 |
| Patagonia | **40**, p69 |
| Patricks | **105**, p134 |
| Pear Tree | **63**, p92 |
| Penbontbren | **128** p157 |
| Pen Bryn Bach | **2**, p31 |
| Penhelig Arms | **4**, p33 |
| Penmaenuchaf Hall | **117**, p146 |
| Pen-y-Dyffryn | **112**, p141 |
| Peterstone Court | **83**, p112 |
| Plas Bodegroes | **122**, p151 |
| Porth Tocyn | **10**, p39 |
| Portmeirion | **121**, p150 |
| Priory | **28**, p57 |

## R

| | | |
|---|---|---|
| Raglan Arms | **74**, p103 |
| Ramsey House | **136**, p165 |
| Redberth Lodge | **124**, p153 |
| Richard's | **78**, p107 |

## S

| | | |
|---|---|---|
| Sands Bar & Brasserie | **55**, p84 |
| Seeds | **80**, p109 |
| Seiont Manor | **85**, p114 |
| Ship Inn | **123**, p152 |
| St Brides | **129**, p158 |
| St Tudno | **79**, p108 |
| Stable Door | **67**, p96 |
| Stone Hall | **149**, p178 |
| Stonemill | **126**, p155 |

## T

| | | |
|---|---|---|
| Talkhouse | **118**, p147 |
| Tan-y-Foel | **19**, p48 |
| Thyme Bistro | **44**, p73 |
| Tides | **41**, p70 |
| Tipple 'n' Tiffin | **23**, p52 |
| Tregynon Farmhouse | **119**, p148 |
| Tŷ Mawr | **20**, p49 |
| Tyddyn Llan | **76**, p105 |

Carlton House

## W

| | | |
|---|---|---|
| Walnut Tree Inn | **8**, p37 |
| Warpool Court | **137**, p166 |
| Waterfront | **146**, p175 |
| Welcome to Town Inn | **84**, p113 |
| West Arms | **68**, p97 |
| Windsor Lodge | **143**, p172 |
| Woods Brasserie | **42**, p71 |

| | | |
|---|---|---|
| Wye Knot | **45**, p74 |
| Wynnstay | **95**, p124 |

## Y

| | | |
|---|---|---|
| Y Bistro | **69**, p98 |
| Ye Olde Bull's Head | **17**, p46 |
| Ynshir Hall | **96**, p125 |
| Yr Hen Dafarn | **88**, p117 |

# Vote for your favourite restaurant

**One of the most frequently asked questions concerning Dining out in Wales is 'how do you select the restaurants for inspection?'**

Each edition of Dining out in Wales includes blank Report Forms. Readers are invited to become food critics and are asked to write about meals they have loved or loathed on these forms and enclose a receipt to prove that they actually ate the meal they have written about.

When the completed forms are received they are considered by the inspection team and, if necessary, copies of menus obtained or information acquired from web sites to give an indication of the types of menu offered. If the menu shows promise then an inspector will be sent to check it out. And it's not just restaurants we visit – we are happy to consider inspecting anywhere where good food is served to the public without the need to book overnight accommodation. Garden centres, major attractions and even departmental stores, for example, can offer high quality, good value food that deserves publicity.

And it's not just the food we want to hear about. Tell us about the whole dining experience – was the service enthusiastic, well informed, friendly? Did you feel comfortable in your surroundings – were they clean and well cared for, busy, well lit, pretty? Take a look at the reviews which our inspectors have written and try to provide similar style information on the Report Form.

So next time you dine out in Wales, please let us know what you thought of the experience on one of the Report Forms enclosed in this issue. We promise to consider any recommendations we receive.

Many thanks in anticipation of your contribution.

# Report forms
## Dining out in Wales 2006

To: Dining out in Wales, Welsh Development Agency, Plas Glyndŵr, Kingsway, Cardiff CF10 3AH, Wales, UK

**(PLEASE COMPLETE IN BLOCK CAPITALS)**

Your name (Mr/Mrs/Miss/Ms)

Your address

Postcode

Your email

Telephone

In my opinion the following establishment should/should not* be included in the 2006 issue of Dining out in Wales:
* Delete as appropriate

Name of establishment

Address

Postcode

Meal consumed: Lunch/Dinner*     Date of visit:

Number of people dining

Please attach bill where possible or provide details of cost excluding wine.

**Report**

continued overleaf

# Report forms
## Dining out in Wales 2006

**Reports received before 1st June 2005 will be considered when researching the 2006 edition**

I have no connection with the owners, management or staff of the establishment named and have not been asked by them to submit this report to Dining out in Wales.

Signed                              Date

# Report forms
## Dining out in Wales 2006

Armless Dragon

To: Dining out in Wales, Welsh Development Agency, Plas Glyndŵr, Kingsway, Cardiff CF10 3AH, Wales, UK

**(PLEASE COMPLETE IN BLOCK CAPITALS)**

Your name (Mr/Mrs/Miss/Ms)

Your address

Postcode

Your email

Telephone

In my opinion the following establishment should/should not* be included in the 2006 issue of Dining out in Wales:
* Delete as appropriate

Name of establishment

Address

Postcode

Meal consumed: Lunch/Dinner*        Date of visit:

Number of people dining

Please attach bill where possible or provide details of cost excluding wine.

**Report**

continued overleaf

# Report forms
## Dining out in Wales 2006

Harbourmaster

**Report Forms**

_____
_____
_____
_____
_____
_____
_____
_____
_____
_____
_____
_____
_____
_____
_____
_____

**Reports received before 1st June 2005 will be considered when researching the 2006 edition**

I have no connection with the owners, management or staff of the establishment named and have not been asked by them to submit this report to Dining out in Wales.

Signed                                    Date

# Report forms
## Dining out in Wales 2006

To: Dining out in Wales, Welsh Development Agency, Plas Glyndŵr, Kingsway, Cardiff CF10 3AH, Wales, UK

**(PLEASE COMPLETE IN BLOCK CAPITALS)**

Your name (Mr/Mrs/Miss/Ms)

Your address

Postcode

Your email

Telephone

In my opinion the following establishment should/should not* be included in the 2006 issue of Dining out in Wales:
* Delete as appropriate

Name of establishment

Address

Postcode

Meal consumed: Lunch/Dinner*        Date of visit:

Number of people dining

Please attach bill where possible or provide details of cost excluding wine.

**Report**

continued overleaf

# Report forms
## Dining out in Wales 2006

Plas Bodegroes

Report Forms

_____
_____
_____
_____
_____
_____
_____
_____
_____
_____
_____
_____
_____
_____
_____
_____

**Reports received before 1st June 2005 will be considered when researching the 2006 edition**

I have no connection with the owners, management or staff of the establishment named and have not been asked by them to submit this report to Dining out in Wales.

Signed                                    Date